TAKASHI'S **NOODLES**

TAKASHI'S NOODLES

Takashi Yagihashi WITH HARRIS SALAT
PHOTOGRAPHY BY Tyllie Barbosa

TEN SPEED PRESS
Berkeley | Toronto

Ten Speed Press
PO Box 7123
Berkeley, California 94707
www.tenspeed.com

Distributed in Australia by Simon and Schuster Australia, in Canada by Ten Speed Press Canada, in New Zealand by Southern Publishers Group, in South Africa by Real Books, and in the United Kingdom and Europe by Publishers Group UK.

Cover and text design: Toni Tajima
Recipe testing: Jaclyn Kolber
Food styling: Christina Zerkis
Food stylist assistance: Jaclyn Kolber
Prop styling: Kelly McKaig
Photography assistance: Melissa Romito and
Christy Schmid

Library of Congress Cataloging-in-Publication Data
Yagihashi, Takashi.
Takashi's noodles / Takashi Yagihashi with Harris Salat; photography by Tyllie Barbosa.
      p. cm.
Includes index.
Summary: "A collection of 75 recipes from James Beard Award–winning chef Takashi Yagihashi for both traditional and inventive hot and cold Japanese noodle dishes" —Provided by publisher.
ISBN 978-1-58008-965-4
1. Cookery (Pasta) 2. Noodles—Japan. 3. Cookery, Japanese. I. Salat, Harris. II. Title.
TX809.M17Y34 2009
641.8'22—dc22

                                        2008041473

Printed in China
First printing, 2009

1 2 3 4 5 6 7 8 9 10 — 13 12 11 10 09

Contents

Acknowledgments

From the time I was a child growing up in Mito, Japan, noodles have been close to my heart, like my family and friends. Thank you to all of them for making this book happen.

My heartfelt thanks and gratitude to my father, Sakae, my mother, Tamiko, and my sister, Masumi. And thanks to my wife, Kathy, and my children, Brandon, Emily, and Bridget.

And many thanks to the following people, whose contributions also helped to make this book a reality: the staff at Takashi Restaurant and Takashi's Noodles at Macy's; the Yamasho staff; and Courtney Kaplan, Ken Kido, Reiko Sagioka, and Atsuko Uchida.

Thanks to my brother-in-law, Norio, for inspiring me, and to Jun-san for allowing me to work in your amazing noodle shop.

you need. Dried soba and udon are another option. Dried soba takes 3 to 4 minutes to cook, while dried udon will take longer. Be sure to follow package instructions for exact cooking times. With udon, by the way, I use two styles (there are many), *sanuki*, which is like thick spaghetti, and *inaniwa*, which resembles linguine. Finally, you can also make soba from scratch, which takes a little work, but the taste is incomparable. Please see my recipe on page 38.

Somen. These noodles are usually sold dried. Vermicelli-like somen cooks extremely fast—in about a minute. Follow package instructions for the exact cooking time.

Other Asian Noodles. I use two kinds of Asian noodles in this book: rice noodles and bean thread noodles. Rice noodles are sold dried and come in a wide variety of styles. For my recipes, stick to the rice noodles that look like fettuccine. Bean thread noodles are also sold dried and are called *harusame* in Japanese markets or *saifun* in Asian markets. They both cook quickly. Be sure to follow package instructions for exact cooking times.

Pasta. Italian noodles abound everywhere, of course. Try to find pasta actually made in Italy, if possible; the taste is often better. I like store-bought fresh noodles, too, which are easily available. And if you have a pasta maker, follow my instructions for fresh Egg Pasta (page 112), which I use in a number of dishes.

COOKING NOODLES

There are a couple of rules for cooking noodles. First, make sure you cook Japanese and Asian noodles in plenty of plain, unsalted water in a pot large enough to hold 4 quarts. For pasta, add 3 tablespoons of salt to the 4 quarts of water. Noodles need a lot of room to swim around in the pot while they boil, so they all cook through evenly.

Now, whether you're preparing fresh or dried noodles, keep in mind that all cooking times are approximate—you have to taste them for doneness. Like Italians, Japanese enjoy their noodles cooked al dente (what we call *koshi*). When I was growing up, my mother taught me an easy way to check if noodles are ready, a technique I still use today: simply pull a couple of noodles out of the cooking pot with chopsticks or tongs, run them under cold water, and bite into them. They should be tender and cooked through, but not mushy. Don't hesitate to check for doneness several times while your noodles are cooking.

COOLING DOWN NOODLES

If you're preparing one of my cold noodle recipes, here's how to cool just-cooked noodles so they keep their flavor and firm texture: First, prepare an ice bath. Next, get a colander ready in the sink. Once the noodles are cooked quickly drain them into the colander and rinse under plenty of cold running water. At first, this water may appear slightly milky, because noodles can give off excess surface starch. Once the water turns clear, you're done. Next, place the noodles in the ice bath, which is simply a mixing bowl filled with water and lots of ice, for 30 seconds. When they're cool, remove them by hand, squeezing the noodles gently to shed any excess water. Transfer them to a plate and top with a few ice cubes so they keep cool. (You can let the ice slowly melt over the noodles.)

BLANCHING AND SHOCKING VEGETABLES

Throughout the book, you'll see that I ask you to quickly cook vegetables in boiling water, then just as quickly cool them in an ice bath. Why? This technique is what we chefs call "blanching and shocking." By boiling vegetables for 30 seconds to 1 minute *before* you cook them further, you're removing any bitterness and raw taste from the ingredient and concentrating its natural flavor. Placing the vegetables in an ice bath immediately after boiling stops the process instantly, hence, the "shock." Be sure not to actually cook the ingredient at this stage—you're just lightly blanching it. Also, before starting to blanch, be sure to have an ice bath ready.

DASHI

Dashi, or stock, plays a vitally important role in Japanese cooking. For most of its history, Japan was a society that did not consume meat or poultry, relying only on vegetables and seafood. As a result, the butter and animal fats found in Western cuisine did not exist in Japan. Instead, we relied on dashi as the fundamental flavoring agent of our food. I cook with dashi throughout this book. Although dashi is made from a variety of ingredients, in the recipes that follow I rely on the classic combination of dried shaved bonito and dried kelp.

Preparing dashi from scratch is not difficult, but if you're pressed for time, you can also use "dashi packs." These packs look like large tea bags and contain the ingredients in powdered form. All you do is drop it into a pot of cold water, bring it to a boil, and simmer. (Follow package instructions for exact cooking times.) Toss the used pack, and you're done. They're fast, efficient, and economical, and they can sit on your shelf for months. You can find dashi packs in Japanese markets and online. There are a few types, but stick to the "kombu and katsuobushi" variety (kelp and bonito) for my recipes.

One final note: you might come across instant dashi products, much like powdered soup bouillon, in your supermarket. Avoid them. They're loaded with artificial ingredients, and I never use them.

EATING NOODLES, JAPANESE STYLE

Finally, here's the most important advice I can give you when eating Japanese noodles: slurp loudly! There's a practical reason for this: when you're eating hot noodles, slurping cools the noodles as they enter your mouth, so you can consume them quickly, as they taste best when they're hottest. With cold noodles, slurping helps you suck up not just the noodle but also the cold sauce that accompanies it. Back in Japan, it's remarkable to listen to the sounds of a typical ramen shop during the lunchtime rush: besides the clanking of pots and pans and calling out of orders, it's usually eerily quiet—except for the sounds of customers slurping at full volume. Take a page out of their book and slurp away.

CHAPTER ONE | Ramen

RAMEN

RAMEN is Japan's ultimate comfort food, the equivalent of a cheeseburger, fried chicken, and deep-dish pizza rolled into one. Chinese immigrants first popularized these hearty wheat noodles, originally from their homeland, in the late nineteenth century. The Japanese quickly adopted them. The first modern ramen shop opened its doors in Japan in 1910, and after that—look out: ramen exploded in popularity, and today there are tens of thousands of ramen shops dotting the country. There are ramen-related books and magazines, the *Ramen Explorer* TV show, a "Ramen Stadium" featuring top noodles from across the country, and a theme attraction called the "Ramusement Park." Some ramen shops even have cult followings, patronized by the "ramen *otaku*"— the ramen obsessed—who find them through a 10,000-plus online Ramen Bank accessible by mobile phone.

So why all this excitement over a bowl of noodles?

When we think of ramen in America, what usually comes to mind are those just-add-water bricks of instant dried noodles, the cheap snack that fueled a thousand college all-nighters. But in Japan, ramen is different.

In high school, my favorite ramen shop was an eight-seat hole-in-the-wall called Kinrukan—and I couldn't get enough of it. I must have eaten there at least five times a week, especially after baseball practice. The place was always packed. A handwritten paper stuck to the wall announced the menu. Smoke poured out of the kitchen in the back—ventilation was iffy—but that aroma made me even more ravenous. Kinrukan specialized in classic "Tokyo-style" ramen, where noodles are served in a soy sauce–flavored chicken stock and finished with slices of barbecued pork, marinated bamboo shoots, sliced fish cake, and sliced hard-boiled eggs. I can still picture that steaming bowl of noodles with its deeply satisfying broth and heavenly soy sauce fragrance. Thirty years later, it's still seared in my memory, a taste I'll never forget. Deftly prepared, these down-home noodles embody everything that Japanese cuisine is about: a sublime combination that is so much more than the sum of its parts.

Ramen is a dish you typically go out to enjoy rather than make yourself. The different regions of Japan are intensely proud of their local recipes, from the rich, miso-based ramen of the far north to the hearty pork-stock variety famous in the country's south. I love all styles, and enjoy them the way Japanese typically do—as a filling lunch or a midnight snack after a night out with friends. When I was a college student in Tokyo, I was hard-pressed to find an open seat at my favorite ramen shop at 2 A.M.!

When I moved to Chicago some twenty years ago, though, I had a problem: a good bowl of ramen was impossible to find. But I couldn't live without my beloved noodles. So, being a chef, I naturally started to cook them at home— and I realized how easy it is to prepare delicious, authentic ramen yourself. I know you'll agree when you try my recipes in this chapter. In addition to the traditional broth-based preparations, I'm including a number of terrific stir-fried and cold ramen dishes that I make for my family, which are perfect for quick summer meals.

Ramen Chicken Stock

Makes 4 quarts

This is the basic and versatile chicken stock I use for my ramen recipes, and it is flavored with Japanese ingredients. You can prepare a big batch and store any extra in the freezer.

4 quarts water

4 pounds chicken bones

1¾ cups peeled and chopped carrots

1½ cups chopped celery

1 cup chopped leek, white part only

¼ green cabbage

½ head garlic, halved horizontally

1 (1-inch) piece ginger, smashed

1 piece kombu, wiped with a damp cloth

½ cup sake

Combine the water and chicken bones in a large, 10-quart stockpot. Set it over high heat and bring the water to a boil. Skim the surface well to remove any impurities.

Add the carrots, celery, *negi*, cabbage, garlic, ginger, kombu, and sake. Decrease the heat to low and simmer for 2 hours. Add more water as needed to keep the liquid at the same level.

Strain the stock well through a fine-mesh sieve.

and balsamic vinegar. Mix until the butter melts and the Parmesan cheese is well incorporated.

Place a large pot of salted water over high heat and bring to a boil. Add the spaghetti and cook, following package instructions. Drain well and divide the noodles among 4 plates.

While the noodles are cooking, finish the sauce by adding the salt, pepper, nutmeg, cayenne pepper, and basil. Adjust the seasonings to taste.

To serve, ladle ½ cup of bolognese sauce over each plate of spaghetti.

Medley of Japanese Mushrooms with Orecchiette

Serves 4

This is one of my favorite dishes for a dinner party or family get-together: it's foolproof, makes a beautiful presentation, and everyone will love the layers and layers of flavor. I use cultivated mushrooms in this recipe, so you can cook it year-round. Orecchiette, which is sometimes referred to as "little ears pasta," is a famous pasta of the Puglia region of southern Italy, and the ideal shape to hold the creamy sauce.

8 ounces dried orecchiette

2 tablespoons thinly sliced bacon (about 1 piece)

1 tablespoon extra-virgin olive oil

1 tablespoon thinly sliced garlic

3 tablespoons minced shallots

4 tablespoons (¼ cup or ½ stick) unsalted butter

12 shiitake mushrooms, ends removed, sliced ¼ inch thick

1 cup shimeji mushrooms, ends trimmed

2 cups stemmed and halved enoki mushrooms

1 cup heavy cream

½ cup grated Parmesan cheese

1 teaspoon kosher salt

Pinch of pepper

1 tablespoon minced parsley, plus a few parsley leaves for garnish

Place a large pot of salted water over high heat and bring to a boil. Add the orecchiette and cook, following package instructions. Drain well.

Prepare the sauce while the orecchiette is cooking. Set a large sauté pan over medium-high heat. Add the bacon and cook until crisp, stirring frequently, 3 to 4 minutes. Add the olive oil, then the garlic and shallots and cook, stirring constantly, until the shallots are soft and the garlic is just beginning to turn golden brown, about 1 minute.

Stir in the butter. Once it has melted, add all the mushrooms and cook until they become soft, about 4 minutes. Stir in the orecchiette, cream, and Parmesan cheese until well combined, then add the salt, pepper, and minced parsley. Mix well and remove the pan from the heat.

To serve, divide the pasta and sauce among 4 plates. Garnish with the parsley leaves.

Smoked Salmon and Salmon Roe Fettuccine

Serves 4

Salmon roe, a sushi bar standard here in America, is a very popular ingredient in Japan. I love how these orange-colored pearls explode with a burst of flavor when you bite into them. They add a wonderful zing to this classic fettuccine recipe. Try this dish in the spring when broccoli is at its peak.

¼ cup pine nuts

2 cups broccoli florets

1 cup thinly sliced fennel bulb

12 ounces dried fettuccine noodles

2 tablespoons extra-virgin olive oil

3 tablespoons unsalted butter

½ cup thinly sliced red onion

Pinch each of salt and pepper

6 ounces sliced smoked salmon, cut into bite-size pieces

8 cherry tomatoes, quartered

¼ cup chopped chives (2-inch lengths)

16 (2-inch-long) Parmesan shavings (use a vegetable peeler on a block of Parmesan)

2 tablespoons salmon roe caviar

Preheat the oven to 350°F. Spread the pine nuts on a baking sheet and roast in the oven until lightly toasted, about 5 minutes. Set aside.

Prepare an ice bath and place a large pot of salted water over high heat. When the water reaches a boil, add the broccoli and fennel and cook for 1 minute. Remove the vegetables with a slotted spoon (don't drain the water), and submerge them in the ice bath for 30 seconds. Remove the vegetables from the water and pat them dry with a paper towel. Set aside.

Bring the same pot of water to a boil again. Add the fettuccine noodles and cook, following package instructions. Drain well and set aside.

Heat a large sauté pan over medium heat. Add the olive oil and butter. Once the butter has melted, stir in the onion and cook for 30 seconds, then add the cooked broccoli and fennel. Sauté the vegetables for 2 minutes, then increase the heat to high and mix in the cooked pasta. Cook for 1 minute longer, stirring frequently, then turn off the heat and season with the salt and pepper.

To serve, divide the pasta and vegetables among 4 plates. Top each with one-fourth of the smoked salmon, followed by the cherry tomatoes, chives, Parmesan shavings, toasted pine nuts, and salmon roe.

Spaghetti with Razor Clams, Seaweed, and Tomato-Basil Sauce

Serves 4

This dish brings back memories of my childhood. I grew up only ten miles from the coast, and spent many Sunday mornings with my friends on the beach digging for clams, which we'd bring home to cook. I love the dense, chewy texture of razor clams, but if they're not available, other clams work great with this recipe, too, including Manila, Asari, and littleneck.

TOMATO-BASIL SAUCE

Makes 2 cups

6 Roma tomatoes

¼ cup extra-virgin olive oil

3 tablespoons minced shallot

1 tablespoon minced garlic

½ cup diced red bell pepper

¼ cup tomato paste

1½ teaspoons sugar

2 teaspoons balsamic vinegar

¼ cup minced basil leaves

2 teaspoons salt

Pinch of pepper

SPAGHETTI WITH RAZOR CLAMS AND SEAWEED

1 pound razor clams, alive and in shells (can be found in fish markets or Asian grocery stores; or substitute with any type of shellfish)

3 tablespoons dried wakame

2 cups hot water

12 ounces dried spaghetti

2 tablespoons unsalted butter

2 tablespoons extra-virgin olive oil

Pinch each of salt and pepper

To make the sauce, prepare a small ice bath and bring a pot of water to a boil. With a paring knife, remove the core from the tomatoes and lightly score an X on the bottoms. Blanch the tomatoes in a two-step process: add 1 tomato to the boiling water for 10 seconds, then remove and submerge in the ice bath for 10 seconds. Now add this same tomato to the boiling water again, this time for 5 seconds, and then submerge in the ice bath until cold. Drain. Repeat with the remaining 5 tomatoes.

Once chilled, peel the skins off the tomatoes with a paring knife, then cut the tomatoes into quarters. Use the paring knife to remove and discard the seeds, then chop the tomatoes into small pieces.

Heat 2 tablespoons of the olive oil in a pot over medium heat. Add the shallot, garlic, and bell pepper and cook, stirring frequently, for 10 minutes, or until soft. Stir in the chopped tomatoes and the remaining 2 tablespoons olive oil and increase the heat to high. Once the liquid starts to boil (the tomatoes will release a lot of water), cook for 5 minutes, then stir in the tomato paste. Cook for 1 to 2 minutes longer, until tomato paste is well incorporated, then stir in the sugar, balsamic vinegar, basil, and salt and pepper. Adjust the seasonings to taste.

To make the spaghetti with razor clams, prepare the clams by cutting the shell with a paring knife. Remove the meat, keeping the pieces as whole as possible. Rinse well in salted water to remove any sand, then wash under cold running water for a few minutes. Cut the clams into 1-inch pieces and refrigerate until ready to use.

In a bowl, cover the wakame with the hot water and let sit for 10 minutes. Drain well and set aside.

Place a large pot of salted water over high heat and bring to a boil. Add the spaghetti noodles and cook, following package instructions. Drain well and return the noodles to the pot. Stir in the butter.

Place a sauté pan over high heat and add the olive oil. When the oil just begins to smoke, add the clams and season with the salt and pepper. Cook for 15 seconds, turn over the clams, season again with salt and pepper, and cook for 15 seconds longer. Remove the pan from the heat.

To serve, divide the noodles among 4 plates and top each with ½ cup of the sauce, then the wakame and clams.

Spaghetti with Spicy Mentaiko

Serves 4

This is *the* iconic Japanese pasta dish, the dish that popularized the notion of combining Italian pasta with intrinsically Japanese ingredients, in this case, *mentaiko*, aromatic *obha* leaves, and crispy nori. This spaghetti is as popular at home as it is in *"wafu pasta"* restaurants, places specializing in Japanese-style pasta.

12 ounces dried spaghetti

4 tablespoons (¼ cup or ½ stick) unsalted butter

½ cup mentaiko (spicy fish roe), membrane removed

¼ cup mayonnaise

8 obha leaves, halved and thinly sliced

2 teaspoons lemon juice

Pinch each of salt and pepper

1 sheet nori, thinly sliced, or ¼ cup shredded nori

Place a large pot of salted water over high heat and bring to a boil. Add the spaghetti and cook, following package instructions. Drain well and set aside.

Heat a sauté pan over medium heat. Add the butter. When the butter melts, stir in the *mentaiko* and cook for 30 seconds, then add the spaghetti and mayonnaise. Stirring constantly, cook until all the ingredients are well combined, 1 to 2 minutes. Mix in the *obha* leaves, lemon juice, and salt and pepper.

To serve, divide the pasta among 4 plates and garnish with the nori.

Squid-Ink Pasta with Crabmeat-Stuffed Squid

Serves 4

This dish first caught my eye early in my career when I worked as a line cook at Chicago's legendary Ambria Restaurant. We served it as an appetizer, making everything from scratch, including the pasta—and it was one of our most popular dishes. This is a perfect dish for dinner parties. I promise it will impress your guests. Follow the fresh Egg Pasta recipe on page 109, making sure you include the optional squid ink.

STUFFED SQUID

8 pieces squid, cleaned

1½ cups crabmeat, picked over to remove any cartilage

⅛ teaspoon kosher salt

Pinch of pepper

2 teaspoons chopped fresh basil

2 teaspoons chopped fresh tarragon

2 teaspoons minced shallots

4 toothpicks

2 tablespoons extra-virgin olive oil

2 tablespoons unsalted butter

WHITE WINE SAUCE

2 tablespoons minced shallots

½ teaspoon minced garlic

2 teaspoons lemon juice

⅔ cup dry white wine

⅔ cup heavy cream

⅔ cup grated Parmesan cheese

1 tablespoon minced chives

4 servings fresh Egg Pasta with squid ink, cut into spaghetti (page 109)

Salt and pepper

To make the squid, preheat the oven to 450°F and bring a large pot of salted water to a boil. Slice 4 of the squid into ¼-inch-thick rings and set aside.

Combine the crabmeat, salt, pepper, basil, tarragon, and shallots in a bowl. Using your fingers, fill the 4 uncut pieces of squid with the stuffing, two-thirds of the way full. Close the openings of each piece of stuffed squid with a toothpick by making a sewing stitch.

Place a large nonstick ovenproof pan over high heat and add the olive oil. When the oil just begins to smoke, place the stuffed squid in the pan and decrease the heat to medium. Cook until the bottom of the squid turns golden brown, about 3 minutes, then flip the squid over and add the butter to the pan. Cook for 2 minutes, then place the pan in the oven and cook for 2 minutes longer. Remove the pan from the oven and place the squid on a plate. Cover and keep warm.

To make the sauce, drain the oil from the pan and return it to the stove top over medium heat. Add the shallots, garlic, lemon juice, and white wine, and simmer until most of the liquid evaporates, about 6 minutes. Add the cream and Parmesan cheese. Cook for 1 minute, then stir in the chives and reserved sliced squid and cook for 30 seconds longer. Remove the pan from the heat and cover to keep warm.

Place a large pot of water over high heat and bring to a boil. Add the pasta and cook for 2 minutes. Drain. Return the pan with the sauce to medium heat, add the pasta, and season to taste with salt and pepper. Cook until the pasta is well combined, about 1 minute.

To serve, divide the pasta among 4 plates. Top each with one piece of stuffed squid, then spoon the sliced squid and sauce over the top. Serve hot.

Potato Gnocchi in Lemon-Butter Sauce with Scallops and Sea Urchin

Serves 4

Sea urchin, or *uni* in Japanese, is a favorite delicacy back home, one that can be enjoyed raw or mixed as a dressing for seafood. I love the creamy, rich texture and sweet flavor of sea urchin combined with the lemony butter sauce of this gnocchi dish. You can prepare the gnocchi ahead of time, if you'd like. Just toss it with 1 tablespoon olive oil and refrigerate for up to 5 days or freeze for up to 1 month.

GNOCCHI

1 pound russet potatoes (about 2 large potatoes)

1 egg

1 egg yolk

1/3 cup grated Parmesan cheese

1/2 tablespoon extra-virgin olive oil

2 teaspoons kosher salt

1 1/4 cups all-purpose flour, plus more for dusting

SCALLOPS, PEAS, AND SEA URCHIN

2 tablespoons extra-virgin olive oil

8 ounces bay scallops, trimmed

2 tablespoons unsalted butter

1/2 cup grated Parmesan cheese

1/2 cup spring peas (thawed if using frozen)

Pinch each of salt and pepper

20 pieces sea urchin

LEMON-BUTTER SAUCE

4 tablespoons (1/4 cup or 1/2 stick) unsalted butter

2 tablespoons lemon juice

2 tablespoons minced parsley

Pinch each of salt and pepper

To make the gnocchi, preheat the oven to 425°F. Use a fork to poke holes in the potatoes, then put them on a baking sheet. Roast the potatoes in the oven until very soft, about 2 hours. Remove from the oven and let cool at room temperature for 15 minutes, or until just cool enough to handle.

While the potatoes are still hot, carefully cut them in half and use a spoon to scoop out the insides. Discard the skins. Grind the potatoes through a ricer or mash with a handheld potato masher until no lumps remain. Use a rubber spatula to stir in the egg, egg yolk, Parmesan cheese, olive oil, and kosher salt.

With your hands, slowly mix in the 1 1/4 cups flour until well combined. Divide the dough into 4 pieces.

Roll 1 piece of dough on a lightly floured surface into a long, 1/2-inch-thick rope. Gently pinch one end of the dough with your thumb and forefinger, and cut. The piece will resemble a small pillow. Keep pinching and cutting the dough into 1-inch-long pieces and place them on a large plate dusted with flour. Repeat the process with the remaining 3 pieces of dough.

Prepare an ice bath, then place a large pot of salted water over high heat and bring to a boil. Add one-fourth of the gnocchi to the boiling water and slightly decrease the heat. Simmer the gnocchi for 1 1/2 to 2 minutes, or until they float to the surface, then remove the gnocchi and submerge them in the ice bath for 30 seconds. Drain the gnocchi and set aside on a plate. Repeat until all the gnocchi are cooked through and cooled.

To prepare the scallops, peas, and sea urchin, set a sauté pan over high heat. Pour the olive oil into the pan and when it just begins to smoke, carefully add the scallops. Cook for 20 to 30 seconds, or just long enough for the bottoms of the scallops to caramelize and turn golden brown. Flip the scallops over and cook on the other side for 30 seconds. Remove the scallops and set them on a plate. Cover to keep warm.

Add the butter to the sauté pan and set over high heat. Once the butter melts, add the gnocchi and mix well. Cook for 1 minute, then stir in the Parmesan cheese and spring peas. Add the sautéed scallops and season with the salt and pepper. Toss all the ingredients together and remove the pan from the heat. Divide the gnocchi and scallops among 4 plates. Top each with 5 pieces of sea urchin and set aside.

To prepare the sauce, return the sauté pan to high heat and add the butter. Once the butter just begins to turn brown, stir in the lemon juice, then the parsley and salt and pepper.

Pour the sauce over the gnocchi and serve.

Fresh Egg Pasta with Pork Loin, Chinese Eggplant, Baby Bok Choy, and Spicy Miso Sauce

Serves 2

What I love about this recipe is how well fresh Italian pasta works combined with these Asian flavors. It's a true crossover dish, the pasta adding wonderful flavor and texture to the earthy and spicy notes in the sauce. Pork and eggplant is a natural combination that reminds me of Sichuan cuisine. Chinese eggplants, by the way, have a delicate skin, so when you peel them you can leave on some strips of skin for aesthetic purposes. This stir-fried dish is unwieldy to cook for four servings, so prepare it in two batches.

SPICY MISO SAUCE

2 tablespoons shiro miso (white miso)

½ teaspoon Japanese soy sauce

1½ tablespoons mirin

½ tablespoon hoisin sauce

½ tablespoon water

½ teaspoon grated ginger

½ teaspoon tobanjan (Chinese chili paste)

½ teaspoon sugar

STIR-FRY

6 tablespoons vegetable oil

1 Chinese eggplant, lightly peeled and cut into ¼-inch-thick rounds, then halved

6 ounces pork loin, thinly sliced

1 clove garlic, thinly sliced

1 baby bok choy, cut into bite-size pieces

½ recipe fresh Egg Pasta, cut into spaghetti noodles (page 109; without optional squid ink), or 6 ounces dried spaghetti

To make the sauce, combine all the ingredients in a bowl and mix well. Set aside.

Place a large pot of salted water over high heat and bring to a boil.

To make the stir-fry, heat 4 tablespoons of the vegetable oil in a large sauté pan over high heat. Add the eggplant and cook until each side is caramelized, about 1½ minutes per side. Transfer to a plate. (*Note:* The eggplant will absorb most of the oil.)

With the oil that's still in the pan, add the pork loin and decrease the heat to medium. Sear each side for 30 seconds, then transfer to the plate with the eggplant.

Decrease the heat to low and add the remaining oil to the pan. Add the sliced garlic to the pan and cook for 30 seconds, stirring constantly. Then mix in the bok choy and cook until it begins to wilt, about 30 seconds longer. Add the reserved eggplant and pork back to the pan along with the miso sauce. Mix well and turn off the heat.

Add the pasta to the boiling water and cook for 2 minutes, or until al dente. Drain well and add the pasta to the sauté pan. Increase the heat to medium and mix quickly with the pork and vegetables until all the ingredients are heated through and well combined. Divide the noodles, pork, and vegetables between 2 plates and serve hot.

CHAPTER SEVEN | # Appetizers

Beef Harumaki

Makes 20 pieces, serves 5

In Japan, these crispy pan-fried rolls run a close second to gyoza as a favorite side dish to a steaming bowl of ramen. *Harumaki* is often prepared with shrimp or pork, but I like using beef, which beautifully complements the layers of flavors in this recipe. Besides, the irresistible combination of beef and peppers reminds me of my adopted hometown of Chicago's famous Italian beef sandwiches. *Harumaki* also freezes well. The trick is to assemble the rolls completely before sticking them in the freezer. You can even fry the *harumaki* while the filling is still frozen. I always keep some frozen rolls on hand for an impromptu midnight snack.

MARINATED BEEF

1 tablespoon sake

1 tablespoon Japanese soy sauce

1 teaspoon sesame oil

1/8 teaspoon black pepper

1/4 teaspoon kosher salt

8 ounces beef tenderloin, skirt, or strip steak, thinly sliced and cut into 2-inch-long pieces

STIR-FRY SAUCE

1 tablespoon Japanese soy sauce

2 tablespoons sake

1 tablespoon hoisin sauce

1 teaspoon sesame oil

1/4 cup Beef Broth (page 107)

2 tablespoons cornstarch

2 tablespoons water

MUSTARD SAUCE

1 tablespoon mustard powder

1 tablespoon cold water

FILLING

1/4 cup vegetable oil

1 cup thinly sliced stemmed shiitake mushrooms (about 6)

1/3 cup thinly sliced canned bamboo shoots

2 stalks celery, peeled, thinly sliced, and cut into 2-inch-long pieces

1 green bell pepper, stemmed, seeded, and thinly sliced

1 red bell pepper, stemmed, seeded, and thinly sliced

10 stalks Broccolini, ends trimmed and halved

10 spring roll sheets, thawed (found in the frozen section of the supermarket)

1 tablespoon flour mixed with 1 tablespoon water ("flour paste")

1/4 cup vegetable oil

Japanese soy sauce

Salt and pepper

To make the beef, in a large bowl, combine the sake, soy sauce, sesame oil, black pepper, and salt. Add the beef and mix well. Cover and refrigerate for 10 minutes.

To make the stir-fry sauce, combine the soy sauce, sake, hoisin, sesame oil, and stock in a bowl. In another bowl, mix together the cornstarch and water. Set aside.

(continued)

To make the mustard sauce, in a small bowl, mix together the mustard powder and water. Set aside.

To make the filling, heat a large sauté pan over high heat. Add 2 tablespoons of the oil. Once the oil is hot but not smoking, carefully add the marinated beef and stir, using a wooden spoon or heat-proof spatula. Continue stirring for 1 minute, then transfer to a bowl.

Using the same pan, heat the remaining 2 tablespoons oil over high heat, then add the mushrooms and bamboo shoots. Cook for 30 seconds, stirring constantly, then add the celery and both bell peppers. Continue cooking, stirring occasionally, until the peppers begin to soften, about 3 minutes. Add the beef back to the pan and mix in the stir-fry sauce; cook for 30 seconds, then stir in the cornstarch mixture and cook for 1 minute, or until the sauce thickens.

Remove the pan from the heat and transfer the filling to a bowl. Refrigerate until it has completely cooled, about 1 hour.

Prepare an ice bath and place a medium pot of salted water over high heat. When the water comes to a boil, add the Broccolini, and cook for 1 minute, then transfer to the ice bath for 10 seconds. Quickly place on paper towels to dry. Set aside at room temperature.

Separate the spring roll sheets and stack them. On an angle, cut off one corner of the sheets, about 1½ inches long (one-sixth of the sheet), and discard the corner. Set 1 sheet in front of you with the cut side closest to you (the pointed end should be farthest away). Cover the remaining sheets with a slightly damp towel to keep them from drying out.

Measure ⅓ cup of the filling and place it on the spring roll sheet, about 1 inch above the bottom. Carefully spread out the mixture so the ingredients lie in the same direction, one next to the other. Be careful to keep the filling at least 1 inch from the sides. Gently begin rolling, lightly squeezing to keep the roll tight. After two turns, press down on the sides to secure the filling and tuck the unfilled edges in. Continue rolling. Secure the top with a small dab of flour paste. Repeat with the remaining 9 spring roll sheets and the filling.

Heat a medium nonstick sauté pan over medium heat and add the oil. Heat for 1 minute, making sure it doesn't get too hot. Add the spring rolls one at a time and cook until the bottoms turn golden brown, about 2 minutes. Then, using tongs, carefully turn the spring rolls over and brown the remaining sides. When done cooking, transfer the spring rolls to a paper towel–lined plate and allow to cool slightly, then cut in half on a diagonal.

To serve, arrange 4 pieces of Broccolini at the end of each of 5 long plates, along with 1 teaspoon of the mustard sauce, followed by 4 spring roll pieces. Serve with the soy sauce and a mixture of salt and pepper on the side. Or, serve sliced in half at a 45 degree angle, paired with gyoza on a serving platter.

Grilled Squid

Serves 4

Grilled squid, the Japanese version of fried calamari, is extremely popular in Japan's neighborhood *izakaya*, or eating pubs. Whenever I order this dish I always think of my mother, who once warned me against eating squid from street vendors. My mom, always looking out for me! Using nice, fresh squid, this dish is simple to prepare and perfect with a cold glass of sake. Try to buy the largest calamari-style squid you can find.

1¼ pounds fresh squid

SAUCE
¼ cup Japanese soy sauce
3 tablespoons mirin
2 tablespoons sake
1 teaspoon grated ginger

24 snow peas, trimmed
Salt
1 teaspoon vegetable oil
Pinch of white sesame seeds
Pinch of ichimi togarashi (Japanese red pepper flakes)

Rinse the squid under cold water. Clean by holding the body in one hand and using the other hand to pull off the head. Remove and discard all materials inside the body until you are left with a hollow tube. Cut just above the eyes on the head to remove and keep the tentacles. Rinse the tubes and tentacles well in cold water. Discard the remaining parts.

To make the sauce, combine the soy sauce, mirin, and sake in a small pan over medium heat and cook until the liquid just comes to a boil. Keep warm until ready to use. Stir in the ginger just before serving.

Prepare an ice bath and place a pot of salted water over high heat. When the water comes to a boil, drop the snow peas in and cook until they turn bright green, about 30 seconds. Remove and submerge in the ice bath. Drain, sprinkle with the salt, and set aside.

To cook the squid, set a grill or grill pan over high heat and brush on a thin layer of the vegetable oil. Season the squid with salt and place on the hot grill. Cook for 2½ to 3 minutes per side, or until cooked through. Note that when you begin cooking the squid, it releases a lot of juices. As soon as the skin turns red and there's no more liquid, it's ready. Be careful not to overcook, as the squid can quickly become tough.

Roll the grilled squid in the sauce to lightly coat. Transfer to a cutting board and cut into ¾-inch pieces. Divide the squid among 4 plates and top each with ½ teaspoon sauce, 6 snow peas, and the sesame seeds and *ichimi togarashi*.

Braised Pork Belly

Serves 4

The elegant preparation I introduce here, braised pork belly served in a "sandwich" with a tangy hoisin sauce, is a mouthwatering appetizer. But this dish is also fundamental to ramen noodle cooking. Sliced, it's a classic topping for ramen noodles. And the braising liquid has many uses. You flavor ramen broth with it; simmer bamboo shoots in it, a classic garnish; and even cook hard-boiled eggs in this liquid, which are then sliced in half and added to a bowl of noodles. (See page 24 in the ramen section for an example.) This recipe takes a little bit of time but is very simple to execute—do not be afraid. In fact, when you're cooking the pork or simmering it in the braising liquid, just set a kitchen timer and forget about it. You don't have to watch it closely.

PORK BELLY

½ tablespoon vegetable oil

9 ounces pork belly

4 cups cold water

½ cup sake

1 (1-inch) piece fresh ginger, peeled and smashed

BRAISING LIQUID

1½ cups cold water

1 cup Japanese soy sauce

¾ cups sugar

1 piece star anise

½ teaspoon whole black peppercorns

1 cinnamon stick

1 (1-inch) piece fresh ginger, peeled and smashed

GARNISHES

¼ head iceberg lettuce

¼ cucumber, thinly sliced on a diagonal

SAUCE

2 tablespoons hoisin sauce

1 teaspoon cold water

1 teaspoon cornstarch

MUSTARD SAUCE

2 teaspoons mustard powder

2 teaspoons water

4 steamed buns (also called "Milk Steamed Bread," available at Asian and Chinese stores), defrosted and halved

To prepare the pork belly, place an 11-inch sauté pan over high heat. Add the vegetable oil and heat until the oil just begins to smoke. Using tongs, carefully place the fatty side of the pork belly in the pan and cook until it turns golden brown, about 2 minutes. Turn the pork belly over and repeat on the other sides until nicely browned all over. Decrease the heat if the oil begins to smoke again.

In a 4-quart saucepan, combine the seared pork belly, the cold water, sake, and smashed ginger, and place over high heat. Bring the liquid to a boil, then decrease the heat; simmer, uncovered, for 45 minutes.

To make the braising liquid, combine all the ingredients in a 4-quart saucepan.

Drain the pork belly and discard the liquid, then add the pork belly to the braising liquid in the saucepan. Bring to a boil, then reduce the heat to a simmer and cover. Braise for 1½ hours, or until the pork belly is very tender.

(continued)

Transfer the pork belly and braising liquid to a container and refrigerate, uncovered, until cool, then cover and chill overnight.

The next day, assemble a steamer on the stove top. You can use a perforated pan, steam basket, or bamboo steamer. Fill the bottom with water, cover, and set over high heat. Decrease the heat to medium once the water comes to a boil.

To prepare the garnishes, discard the outer leaves of the iceberg lettuce. Place 3 large leaves in a bowl of cold water along with the cucumber slices. Set aside. (I like to soak cut vegetables in cold water for 10 minutes because it helps them retain their freshness and crispness.)

To make the sauce, combine ½ cup of the chilled braising liquid and the hoisin sauce in a small saucepan and set over high heat. In a bowl, mix the water and cornstarch until smooth. When the sauce just begins to boil, whisk in the cornstarch and cook briefly, just until the sauce begins to thicken. Make sure that it doesn't thicken too much—the sauce should run in a steady stream when poured. Set aside.

To make the mustard sauce, mix the mustard powder and water in a small bowl. Set aside.

Remove the pork belly from the remaining braising liquid and cut into 8 slices, each ¼ inch thick. (You'll have leftover pork belly after you cut these slices. See below for other uses.) Place the slices in a single layer side by side with the halved buns on a plate small enough to fit in the steamer (don't put the buns directly on the steamer because they will stick to it). If you have a large steamer you can do this in one batch, if your steamer is smaller, just steam the pork belly and buns in several batches. Set the plate in the steamer, cover, and cook for 3 to 4 minutes, or until soft and heated through.

While the pork belly and buns are steaming, finish preparing the garnishes by draining the lettuce and cucumber and patting dry with a towel. Cut the lettuce into pieces the size of the steamed buns and stack in 4 small piles. Top each pile with 2 slices of cucumber.

To serve, assemble a braised pork "sandwich" by placing the lettuce, cucumber, and 2 slices of pork belly on half of a bun. Drizzle the sauce over the meat and top with the other half of the bun. Serve the mustard on the side. Repeat for the remaining 3 buns.

IDEAS FOR LEFTOVER PORK BELLY

Any leftover pork belly and remaining braising liquid can be frozen for up to 2 months. The braising liquid can be used in the Shoyu Ramen broth (page 24) and the pork belly can be used as a garnish for various ramens or for fried rice.

Pork Spareribs

Makes 12 spareribs, serves 4

These irresistible ribs are an import from China that have been adopted—and adapted—by Japanese cooks. I like to prepare them with classic Chinese five-spice seasoning, because I love the rich fragrance and flavors of this mixture of cinnamon, anise seed, star anise, cloves, and ginger. But many cooks in Japan prefer to make the spareribs with simply sansho pepper or freshly ground black pepper and salt (use 1 teaspoon of either pepper with ½ teaspoon of kosher salt). Try these different spice combinations to see which ones you like best!

1 quart vegetable oil

SPARERIBS MARINADE

2 cloves garlic, grated

3 tablespoons mirin

2 tablespoons Japanese soy sauce

¼ teaspoon freshly ground black pepper

2 pounds pork spareribs (12 pieces), separated

CABBAGE SALAD

¼ red cabbage, cored and thinly sliced

½ carrot, peeled and thinly sliced

2 tablespoons rice wine vinegar

¼ cup water

1 tablespoon sesame oil

Dash of hot chili oil

1½ tablespoons sugar

½ teaspoon salt

½ cup potato starch

½ teaspoon freshly ground black pepper

½ teaspoon kosher salt

½ teaspoon Chinese five-spice powder (found in the spice section of the grocery store)

½ cup chopped fresh or canned and drained pineapple

Cilantro leaves

Heat a deep fryer or heavy-bottomed pot with 4 inches of vegetable oil to 300°F.

To make the marinade, combine the garlic, mirin, soy sauce, and pepper in a large bowl. Add the spareribs and turn to coat the ribs well. Cover and refrigerate for 20 minutes.

To make the salad, combine the cabbage and carrots in a bowl. Combine the vinegar, water, sesame oil, chili oil, sugar, and salt in a small pot. Bring to a boil, then pour the liquid over the cabbage and carrots. Mix well and set aside until it cools to room temperature, about 30 minutes.

Remove the ribs from the marinade and wipe off excess marinade. Line a tray with paper towels. Place the potato starch on a plate and dredge the spareribs in the starch to lightly coat. Add half of the ribs to the hot oil. Fry until the ribs are cooked through, 6 to 8 minutes. Remove and set on the paper towel–lined tray to absorb the excess oil, then add the remaining spareribs to the fryer and repeat.

Heat an 11-inch nonstick pan over high heat and add ¼ teaspoon each of the black pepper, salt, and Chinese five-spice powder. Add half of the fried spareribs and cook quickly, 30 seconds to 1 minute, until cooked through, adding more seasoning, if necessary. Repeat with the remaining spareribs and ¼ teaspoon each of spices.

To serve, arrange ¼ cup of the cabbage salad in the center of 4 plates and top with one-fourth of the pineapple pieces and cilantro. Place 3 spareribs around each cabbage salad and serve.

Chicken Tatsuta-Age

Makes 20 pieces, serves 4

America's Deep South isn't the only place that loves fried chicken: *tatsuta-age* is Japan's own delicious version, which my family and I are addicted to! Our fried chicken is marinated with traditional Japanese aromatic flavorings and served with a refreshing and savory slaw. You can enjoy this versatile dish hot and crispy, or pack it for a picnic and eat it at room temperature—it travels extremely well. *Tatsuta-age* is also a perfect leftover food. It keeps in the fridge for several days without losing its flavor, and you can turn the boneless chunks into a delicious sandwich. When I was a kid, my mother often included this fried chicken in my lunchbox, a treat I happily share with my own school-age children today. Don't use the breast for this dish—the legs and thighs have much more flavor. Be sure to keep the skin on, too.

SPICY NAPA CABBAGE SLAW

4 leaves napa cabbage, stemmed

1 carrot, peeled and thinly sliced on a diagonal (⅓ cup)

2 scallions, stemmed and thinly sliced on a sharp diagonal (⅓ cup)

¼ red onion, peeled and thinly sliced

1 tablespoon kosher salt

2 teaspoons tobanjan (Chinese chili paste)

1 tablespoon rice wine vinegar

½ teaspoon Japanese soy sauce

½ teaspoon nam pla (fish sauce)

¼ teaspoon hot chili oil

4 chicken legs and thighs, with bone and skin (about 2½ pounds)

MARINADE

2 cloves garlic, peeled and grated (you can use a microplane or regular grater)

1 teaspoon grated ginger

¼ cup Japanese soy sauce

¼ cup mirin

2 teaspoons sesame oil

Pinch of freshly ground black pepper

6 cups vegetable oil, or enough to fill a pan 3 inches deep (you can also use a deep fryer)

1 cup potato starch

Pinch of kosher salt

2 cups leafy greens

1 lime, cut into 8 pieces

To make the cabbage slaw, trim the bottom of the cabbage leaves. Cut the leaves in half and slice the bottom half into ¼-inch-wide slices. Then cut the top leafy halves into 2-inch-wide pieces. Combine all the cabbage in a bowl and submerge in cold water to wash. Drain well and place in a bowl. Add the carrots, scallions, onion, and salt and mix well (the salt will remove excess moisture from the vegetables). Let sit at room temperature for 20 minutes.

Meanwhile, **prepare the chicken.** Using a sharp knife, separate the thighs from the drumstick by cutting between the joint. Cut the thigh in half lengthwise along the bone. Using a cleaver, chop the piece with the bone in half, resulting in 3 similar-size pieces. Also use the cleaver to cut the drumstick in half. Repeat with the remaining chicken. You should have 20 pieces of chicken when done. Place the chicken in a shallow pan and set aside.

To prepare the marinade, combine all the marinade ingredients in a bowl and mix well. Pour the marinade over the chicken and coat well using your hands. There should be just enough marinade to coat the chicken. Cover and refrigerate for at least 20 minutes, or up to 2 hours.

To finish the slaw, rinse it in cold water three times and strain. Squeeze the slaw between your hands in small batches to remove all the excess water and place in a dry bowl; the cabbage should be wilted. Add the *tobanjan*, vinegar, soy sauce, nam pla, and chili oil. Mix well and refrigerate until ready to use.

To finish the chicken, line a shallow tray with paper towels and set aside. Heat the vegetable oil (or as much as you need for a 3-inch depth) in a heavy-bottomed pot over medium-high heat until the oil reaches 325°F, or fill a deep fryer and set the temperature to 325°F. Place the potato starch in a large bowl and gently toss each piece of chicken until lightly coated. Carefully place half the chicken in the hot oil, being careful not to splatter. Cook until the chicken is nicely browned and begins to rise to the surface, 9 to 11 minutes. Once the chicken is cooked through, remove it from the oil using tongs and place on the paper towel–lined tray. Toss with the kosher salt while still hot. Repeat with the second batch of chicken.

While the chicken is cooking, prepare 4 appetizer plates by placing ½ cup of the leafy greens in one corner. Add ⅓ cup slaw to the center of the plate and set 2 lime wedges next to it. Top with 5 pieces of hot chicken and serve immediately.

REUSING FRYING OIL

The frying oil can be reused. When finished frying the chicken, allow it to sit at room temperature until it has cooled completely, then strain through a fine-mesh sieve into a sealable container and store in the refrigerator for several months.

Chicken Yakitori

Makes 20 pieces, serves 4

Yakitori is one of Japan's most beloved comfort foods; restaurants specializing in these grilled chicken skewers can be found everywhere. Chefs typically work in the open behind a long dining counter, slowly searing chicken over all-natural Japanese oak charcoal. The key word here is "slowly"—the secret to delicious yakitori is to carefully caramelize both the meat *and* the sauce coating it. To achieve this, yakitori chefs grill over moderate heat and alternate turning the skewers and dipping them into *tukedare*, the traditional sweet-savory grilling sauce. The result is a wonderful rich flavor and aroma, and a beautiful deep amber color.

But you don't have to be a professional chef to grill amazing yakitori. This dish is also popular among Japanese home cooks, and my recipe below shows how you, too, can achieve yakitori bliss. These skewers are perfect for a party, picnic, campout, or football tailgate. You can prepare them over a stove-top grill or, even better, on an outdoor barbecue (use natural charcoal for the best flavor). Also, the skewers can be assembled and the *tukedare* sauce prepared a day ahead of time. Finally, you can make a vegetarian version of this dish by substituting the chicken with firm tofu cut into ¾-inch cubes. Skewer the tofu, alternating with whole *shishito* peppers, and follow the instructions below, coating the tofu liberally with the *tukedare*.

TUKEDARE

2 cups Japanese soy sauce

⅓ cup sake

⅓ cup water

4 teaspoons ginger juice (see page 149)

2 tablespoons sesame oil

¼ cup lemon juice

1 (6-inch) piece kombu, wiped with a damp cloth

2 cups sugar

1 teaspoon ichimi togarashi (Japanese red pepper flakes)

YAKITORI

1 (3- to 3½-pound) chicken (or use precut and boned legs, thighs, and breasts)

20 (6-inch) bamboo skewers, soaked in water for 30 minutes

½ onion, cubed

4 shiitake mushrooms, stemmed and cubed

1 scallion, both white and green parts, cut into ½-inch pieces

½ green or red bell pepper, cut into 1-inch squares

½ teaspoon salt

To prepare the *tukedare,* combine the soy sauce, sake, water, ginger juice, sesame oil, lemon juice, kombu, and sugar in a saucepot over high heat. Stir until the sugar dissolves. Bring to a boil, then decrease the heat and simmer until the kombu becomes soft, about 20 minutes. Strain the sauce into a narrow container and mix in the *ichimi togarashi*. Set aside.

To prepare the yakitori, remove the wings from the chicken. Butterfly the middle piece (which has 2 bones), keeping the bone and skin. Thread 2 skewers through both pieces to hold them together, with the skin side down. Set aside.

Next, remove the skin from the remaining chicken and set aside. Remove the bones from the chicken breast, legs, and thighs and cut the meat into 1-inch cubes. Now you're ready to skewer. The trick here is to alternate different combinations of meat and vegetables—have fun with it! To start, thread 3 pieces of dark meat onto a skewer, alternating with some onion and shiitake mushrooms. Be sure to leave at least 1 inch of the skewer uncovered. Now repeat with the chicken breast cubes, this time alternately skewering with scallions and shiitake mushrooms. Next,

try a combination with bell peppers. Repeat until all the skewers are prepared. Finally, don't forget to skewer the chicken skin and chicken liver, both traditional delicacies in Japan. But with these two, do *not* add any vegetables (so the skin and liver can cook uniformly).

Heat a barbecue grill or stove-top grill pan over medium heat. Set several skewers of chicken and vegetables and the skin on the grill so the uncovered parts of the skewers hang over the edge. Flip the yakitori after 2 minutes, then cook 1 minute longer on the other side to sear evenly. Remove and dip the yakitori into *tukedare* to lightly coat (you can also use a pastry brush for this step). Now you're ready to slowly caramelize the sauce and cook the chicken, using the following technique: Return the skewers to the grill and cook for 1 minute. Remove and again dip into the *tukedare*. Return to the grill, turning the skewer to cook the other side for another minute. Repeat these steps until the chicken is cooked through and the sauce is caramelized, 8 to 10 minutes. Remember to grill over lower heat than we typically use to barbecue in America, and grill patiently and slowly. You'll turn and dip the skewers at least four times.

Lightly salt the reserved chicken wings and liver pieces and follow the slow turning technique described above— but do not dip them into the *tukedare*. In Japan, yakitori wings are traditionally grilled only with a salt coating, not with sauce.

Line up the grilled yakitori on a platter and serve.

Fried Oysters

Serves 4

Fried oysters are a staple of *izakaya*, the eating pubs that can be found in every Japanese neighborhood. These kinds of establishments are much more popular than bars, because we typically like to nibble on something while we enjoy a drink. In fact, this dish is one of my favorite complements to a frosty mug of draught beer. You'll see that I don't season the cabbage slaw in this recipe. In Japan, we typically create our own impromptu dressing with the two sauces for the oysters.

CABBAGE SLAW

2 cups packed shredded cabbage (stemmed and sliced as thin as possible in long lengths)

¼ cup thinly sliced red onion

½ carrot, peeled and thinly sliced

12 thin slices cucumber, cut on an angle

TARTAR SAUCE

⅓ cup mayonnaise

½ tablespoon minced capers

2 tablespoons minced cornichons or sweet pickles

½ tablespoon minced chives

½ hard-boiled egg, minced

½ teaspoon lemon juice

Pinch of salt

OYSTERS

1 quart vegetable oil

1 pound shucked large oysters, rinsed well and drained

Salt and white pepper

½ cup all-purpose flour

1 egg, beaten

2 cups panko (Japanese-style breadcrumbs)

GARNISHES

½ lemon, cut into 4 wedges

1 plum tomato, quartered

½ cup tonkatsu sauce (Japanese dipping sauce)

To make the slaw, place the cabbage, red onion, carrots, and cucumber in a bowl under running water for 10 minutes. Drain well. Remove the cucumber slices and reserve. Mix the vegetables and refrigerate the slaw until ready to use.

To make the tartar sauce, combine the mayonnaise, capers, cornichons, chives, and egg in a bowl and mix well. Season to taste with lemon juice and salt.

To make the oysters, heat a deep fryer or pan filled with oil 4 inches deep to 325°F. Line a tray with paper towels.

Season the oysters with salt and white pepper. Set up a breading station in the following order: oysters, bowl of flour, beaten egg, bowl of panko, plate. With one hand, lightly coat an oyster in flour and drop it into the egg. Then, with the other hand, make sure the oyster is coated in egg and wipe off any excess. Transfer the oyster to the panko, making sure it is coated well, and move to the plate with the "flour" hand. Repeat with the remaining oysters.

Carefully place 4 or 5 oysters in the hot oil and cook, flipping halfway through, until the crust turns golden brown, about 6 minutes. Set the oysters on the paper towel–lined tray and lightly sprinkle with salt. Repeat with the remaining oysters.

To serve, place ½ cup of slaw in the corner of a plate and place 3 reserved cucumber slices, 1 lemon wedge, and 1 tomato quarter along one side. Set 4 or 5 fried oysters along the other side, and add 2 tablespoons of the tartar sauce in the corner. Serve with 2 tablespoons of the tonkatsu sauce on the side.

Hiyayako—Chilled Tofu, Traditional Style

Serves 4

This dish is an easy summer favorite prepared with ingredients that every home in Japan has handy in the fridge and cupboard. You can pull it together in less than 10 minutes. Whenever I serve *hiyayako* to my American-born friends, the reaction is always the same: "Amazing!" The creamy tofu and aromatic, flavorful garnishes also pair beautifully with fruity sake or a chilled glass of white wine. Make sure you use soft "silken" tofu—the firmer varieties are only for cooking.

1 (14-ounce) package soft (silken) tofu, rinsed under cold water and patted dry

1 teaspoon grated ginger

1 scallion, both white and green parts, thinly sliced on an angle

2 obha leaves, halved and thinly sliced

¼ cup finely shaved katsuobushi (dried bonito flakes)

Mitsuba leaves (optional)

Daikon sprouts (optional)

Japanese soy sauce

Cut the tofu into quarters, then slice each quarter into 12 equal cubes, but hold them together to retain the original shape. Place each block of cubed tofu in a serving bowl and top with one-fourth of the ginger, scallion, *obha* leaves, and katsuobushi. Garnish with the *mitsuba* leaves and daikon sprouts, if desired. Serve with a small cup of soy sauce.

Gyoza

The funny thing about gyoza is that I never cooked them—until I moved to America. Back home I always went out for these extremely popular, garlic-infused pan-fried dumplings, which have a special place in the hearts of Japanese. When I arrived in America, gyoza was one of the comfort foods I missed the most, so I started cooking them at home. That's when I realized how easy it is to prepare perfect gyoza: they simply need a fragrant, juicy, flavor-packed filling; crispy skin on the bottom and silky skin on top; and a spicy dipping sauce. Now my kids and I love to make homemade gyoza together. This recipe is the classic pork-filled version that I grew up with. Keep in mind that you can conveniently freeze uncooked gyoza for up to a month. To prepare, follow the fry-steam technique below with the *frozen* dumplings—no need to defrost. Just extend the cooking time by 3 minutes. *Note:* You can also prepare this dish without pork belly. Just substitute more ground pork (1 pound total). But I love using pork belly here because it adds so much flavor and richness to the gyoza.

6 ounces pork belly

10 ounces ground pork (I prefer ground pork loin)

MUSTARD SPROUTS

2 teaspoons dry mustard powder

2 teaspoons water

2 teaspoons Japanese soy sauce

2 teaspoons rice wine vinegar

1 teaspoon sugar

2 tablespoons salt

8 ounces bean sprouts

SOY-CHILI DIPPING SAUCE

1/2 cup Japanese soy sauce

1/4 cup rice wine vinegar

1 teaspoon hot chili oil

2 teaspoons sugar

FILLING

7 leaves cabbage

1 1/4 teaspoons kosher salt

1 (3-inch) piece fresh ginger, peeled

1/4 cup chicken stock

2 tablespoons sake

3 tablespoons Japanese soy sauce

2 tablespoons sesame oil

1/2 cup minced garlic chives (discard bottom inch)

1/4 cup minced scallions, both white and green parts

1/2 teaspoon grated garlic (2 cloves)

1/2 tablespoon sugar

Pinch of freshly ground black pepper

1 (10-ounce) package gyoza skins (about 50 skins; I prefer Japanese gyoza skins, but you can use Chinese varieties if necessary)

1 to 1 1/4 cups water

1/3 to 1/2 cup vegetable oil

Grind the pork belly using a meat grinder if you have one, or chop well with a chef's knife (do not use a food processor, which will turn the meat into a paste). Combine in a large bowl with the ground pork and refrigerate.

To make the sprouts, combine the mustard powder, water, soy sauce, vinegar, and sugar in a bowl, mix well, and set aside.

In a pot over high heat, bring 4 cups water and the salt to a boil. Add the bean sprouts. Remove from the heat when the water returns to a boil and the sprouts have floated to the surface. Drain through a fine-mesh strainer and combine with the mustard sauce. Set aside.

To make the dipping sauce, whisk together all the ingredients until the sugar dissolves. Refrigerate until ready to serve.

To make the filling, remove the stems from the cabbage leaves a by cutting a long V shape along the sides of the stems and discard. Arrange the leaves in a pile and cut into thirds lengthwise, then turn horizontally and cut into ⅛-inch-thick pieces. Mix well with ½ teaspoon of the kosher salt in a mixing bowl and let sit at room temperature for 20 minutes (the salt will draw out the excess moisture in the cabbage).

Meanwhile, lay a piece of plastic wrap on the counter and grate the peeled ginger over it. Pull up the sides of the plastic around the pile of ginger to create a small packet. Poke a small hole in the bottom of the packet with the tip of a knife and gently squeeze over a clean bowl to gather the ginger juices; continue squeezing until you have extracted 1 tablespoon of liquid. Mix with the chicken stock, sake, soy sauce, and sesame oil. Set aside.

Use a clean towel to wrap one-third of the cabbage and squeeze over the sink to drain, then place the cabbage on a cutting board. Repeat with the remaining cabbage. Roughly chop the drained cabbage and combine with the garlic chives, scallions, and grated garlic in a bowl.

Remove the pork from the refrigerator and mix well by hand until sticky, being careful to work quickly so the pork doesn't become warm. Slowly mix in the seasoned chicken stock. Once it is well combined, mix in the

cabbage, sugar, the remaining ¾ teaspoon salt, and the pepper.

To assemble, lay a gyoza skin on the counter. Place 1 scant tablespoon of the filling in the center. Using your index finger, run a thin layer of water along half of the inner rim and press both sides together to create a tight seal, forming the shape of a half circle. Make four tucks

(continued)

along the edge of the dumpling and set upright on a plate or baking sheet to create a flat bottom. Repeat with the remaining gyoza skins and filling.

To cook, place a medium nonstick sauté pan over high heat and add 1 tablespoon of the vegetable oil. Add 8 to 10 gyoza to the pan, flat side down. When the bottoms have caramelized, in 1 to 1½ minutes, add ¼ cup of the water and cover with a lid. Decrease the heat to medium and cook, covered, until the water has evaporated, 3 to 4 minutes. Uncover the pan and drizzle 1 teaspoon of the oil on the gyoza and continue to cook until the bottoms become crisp, about 2 minutes. Transfer the gyoza to a serving platter with the browned side on display. Repeat with the remaining gyoza, water, and oil.

To serve, arrange 5 gyoza on an appetizer plate with the browned side facing up. Place ⅓ cup of the mustard bean sprouts next to the gyoza and serve with 2 tablespoons of the dipping sauce in a cup.

Marinated Jellyfish with Cucumber Salad

Serves 4

When I was a kid, my parents really wanted me to try this dish. Jellyfish? No way. Until the fourth grade, that is, when I finally got the courage to taste it. I clearly remember that moment because I was so surprised by how delicious it was. In Japan, jellyfish is sold like Portuguese *bacalhau* (dried salted cod), naturally preserved in salt. In America, it can be found in Asian groceries, stored at room temperature in large tubs of water or in 1-pound packages. Be sure to rinse the jellyfish very well to remove excess salt. This dish is prepared with a very traditional Japanese sweet vinegar marinade, which gives it a nice tangy flavor. I added my own twist and included jicama because I love this root's crunchy texture and delicate sweetness. You can also substitute green papaya for the jicama.

AMAZU MARINADE

1 cup rice wine vinegar

$1/4$ cup Dashi (page 40)

1 tablespoon usukuchi (light-colored Japanese soy sauce)

$1/4$ cup plus 1 teaspoon sugar

1 teaspoon salt

Pinch of ichimi togarashi (Japanese red pepper flakes)

12 ounces cured jellyfish, cut into 3- to 4-inch-long by $1/4$-inch-wide pieces

CUCUMBER SALAD

$3/4$ cucumber, peeled and sliced into very thin 2-inch-long matchsticks

$1/8$ jicama, peeled and sliced into very thin 2-inch-long matchsticks

$1/2$ carrot, peeled and sliced into very thin 1-inch-long matchsticks

GARNISHES

1 tablespoon plus 1 teaspoon sesame oil

$1/2$ teaspoon hot chili oil

$1/2$ teaspoon white sesame seeds

2 scallions, bottom half thinly sliced on a sharp angle

2 sprigs cilantro

To make the marinade, combine all the ingredients in a small saucepan and set over high heat. Bring the mixture to a boil and immediately turn off the heat. Allow the marinade to cool to room temperature.

Prepare an ice bath and set aside. Place the jellyfish in another bowl under cold running water for 20 minutes to remove the excess salt. Bring a pot of water to a boil and quickly blanch the jellyfish, just 1 or 2 seconds. Remove and immediately submerge the jellyfish in the ice bath. Drain well and combine the jellyfish with the marinade. Cover and refrigerate for 2 to 3 hours.

To make the salad, divide the cucumbers among 4 shallow bowls, arranging them in a line in the center. In each bowl, place one-fourth of the carrots and jicama on opposite sides of the cucumber.

Drain the jellyfish from the marinade; reserve the marinade. Top the vegetables with one-fourth of the jellyfish, followed by 2 tablespoons of the reserved marinade, 1 teaspoon of the sesame oil, $1/8$ teaspoon of the chili oil, $1/8$ teaspoon of the sesame seeds, and one-fourth of the scallions. Finish the bowls with 3 or 4 cilantro leaves.

Shrimp Shumai

Makes 24 pieces, serves 4

Shumai is a Chinese import that's a popular dish in casual restaurants, and is also a staple of Japanese homes, where it's enjoyed as a snack or a dinnertime side dish (but never as the main course). Leftovers hold up well and can be polished off the next day, or packed into a lunchbox or picnic basket and eaten at room temperature. You can also freeze uncooked shumai for up to a month. Follow the instructions below to steam frozen shumai—no need to defrost; simply add a couple of minutes to the cooking time.

SOY-MUSTARD SAUCE

1 tablespoon rice wine vinegar

2 tablespoons Japanese soy sauce

1 teaspoon mustard powder

1 teaspoon cold water

FILLING

8 ounces shrimp, peeled and deveined, tails off (you can use frozen 16/20 shrimp)

1 scallion, both white and green parts, minced

¼ cup minced canned and drained water chestnuts

¼ cup minced stemmed shiitake mushrooms

1½ tablespoons lard (or substitute vegetable oil)

2 tablespoons sake

1 teaspoon ginger juice (see page 149)

½ teaspoon sesame oil

1 egg white

1 teaspoon kosher salt

⅛ teaspoon pepper

1 tablespoon potato starch

4 baby bok choy

24 square wonton wrappers/skins

¼ cup vegetable oil

Pinch of salt

1 tablespoon black sesame seeds

To make the soy-mustard sauce, combine all the ingredients in a small bowl and mix well. Set aside.

To make the filling, cut the shrimp into bite-size pieces, then roughly chop until the shrimp become almost paste-like but with some small pieces visible. You can also use a food processor, which will give it a smooth texture, but I prefer the more coarse texture you get from chopping by hand. Transfer the shrimp to a bowl and mix with a spatula until the shrimp become very sticky.

Add the scallions, water chestnuts, and mushrooms to the shrimp and mix well. Then add the following ingredients, mixing well between each addition: lard, sake, ginger juice, sesame oil, and egg white. Finally, mix in the salt, pepper, and potato starch.

Meanwhile, place the baby bok choy in a bowl and cover with cold water; let it sit for 10 to 15 minutes.

To assemble the shumai, lay a wonton skin on the counter (cover the remaining skins with a damp towel to keep them from drying out). Place 1 tablespoon of the filling in the center of the wonton skin. (Soak the spoon in water while you're assembling a shumai. This will make it easier to transfer the filling to the wonton.) Hold the wonton skin with the filling with your fingers and gently press the skin to form a small cup. Set the shumai on a cutting board and turn it clockwise while carefully pressing the sides together, creating a tighter cup. Wet a finger with water and use it to gently smooth the top of the shumai. Repeat with the remaining wonton skins and filling.

To cook the shumai, heat a stove-top steamer over high heat, bringing the water to a boil. Brush the bottom of the steamer basket with a small layer of the vegetable oil and add the shumai, leaving 1 inch of space between each. Cover and cook for 3 minutes, then drain the bok choy and add to the steamer. Cover and cook for 3 minutes longer, or until the shumai are cooked through.

Remove the bok choy from the steamer and gently squeeze inside a towel to remove excess moisture. Top with a pinch of salt. Place each bok choy in the center of 4 small plates and arrange 6 shumai around it. Garnish the plates with a pinch of black sesame seeds and serve with the soy-mustard sauce on the side.

Stuffed Chicken Wings

Serves 8

Although technically an appetizer, these stuffed wings are also a convenient main course at lunch—down two of them and I guarantee you'll be happily full for at least 4 hours. The technique here takes a little practice; don't forget to use a very sharp knife. I promise you, your efforts will be worthwhile: this dish never fails to impress. If you have any leftover rice, you can eat it on its own as a side dish, stuff it into grape leaves for a Mediterranean twist, or steam inside a corn husk for a delicious Japanese-style "tamale."

1½ cups sweet rice (also called "sticky rice" or "mochi rice")

1 cup Dashi (page 40)

2 tablespoons Japanese soy sauce

2 tablespoons mirin

3 shiitake mushrooms, stemmed and thinly sliced

¼ cup thinly sliced carrot

¼ cup thinly sliced bamboo shoots

2 tablespoons peeled and thinly sliced gobo (burdock root; can substitute with salsify)

¼ cup diced abura-age (fried tofu cake)

8 chicken wings

34 pea pods, trimmed

8 slices bacon

BRAISING LIQUID

¼ cup Dashi (page 40)

3 tablespoons Japanese soy sauce

1 tablespoon mirin

Rinse the rice three or four times in cold running water, until the water runs clear. Place in a bowl, cover with water, and soak for 15 minutes. Drain well.

To cook the rice in a rice cooker, combine the rice, dashi, soy sauce, mirin, shiitakes, carrots, bamboo shoots, gobo, and *abura-age* in a rice cooker. Follow the rice cooker settings for sweet rice and cook until done.

To cook the rice on the stove top, combine the rice, dashi, soy sauce, mirin, shiitakes, carrots, bamboo shoots, gobo, and *abura-age* in a pot and place over medium heat. Bring to a boil, about 4 minutes, then cover and cook until no liquid remains visible (don't open the lid too often, just peek), about 3 minutes longer. Decrease the heat to low and cook, covered, for 15 minutes.

While the rice is cooking, remove the bones from the chicken wings by first cutting around the top joint (where it attaches to the body) to loosen the meat. Pull down to release the meat from the bone until you reach the second joint. Use a sharp knife to cut through the joint to loosen the bone, being careful not to puncture the skin. Cut around the second joint to loosen the meat again and pull down to the third joint, cutting between the bones to release them. The wing tip should remain intact. Re-form the meat and skin to resemble the original shape. Repeat with the 7 remaining wings. Refrigerate until ready to stuff.

Prepare an ice bath and place a pot of salted water over high heat. When the water comes to a boil, add the pea pods and cook 1 minute. Remove from the water and submerge in the ice bath. Drain well. Slice 10 pea pods into ¼-inch-thick pieces. Set aside the remaining 24 pea pods for garnish.

Once the rice has finished cooking, place 2 cups of it in a large bowl and let cool to room temperature. Mix in the sliced pea pods. Fill a small bowl with cold water and lightly dip your hands in it before touching the rice (sweet rice is extremely sticky when cooked; the water helps keep the rice from sticking to your hands). Measure ¼ cup rice and stuff inside a hollowed-out chicken wing a little bit at a time, being sure to fill the entire wing. Repeat with the remaining 7 wings.

Once all the wings have been stuffed, wrap each with 1 slice bacon and place them all in a 4-quart saucepan (it should be a snug fit).

To make the braising liquid, combine all the ingredients in a bowl and mix well.

Pour the braising liquid over the chicken wings in the pot. Bring the liquid to a boil over high heat, about 1 minute, then cover. Decrease the heat to medium and cook for 5 minutes. Using tongs, carefully turn over each wing to cook the other side. Put the cover back on and cook for 5 to 6 minutes longer, until the chicken is cooked through.

Let the chicken wings cool to room temperature. Place 1 wing on each of 8 small plates, garnish each with 3 pea pods, and top with 1 tablespoon of the braising liquid.

Sweet and Chili Shrimp

Serves 4

This is a popular dish in Japan that I love to prepare because it has so much going for it: complex sweet and tangy flavors, a heavenly ginger and garlic aroma, and wonderful textures. I've included puffed rice paper "chips" to add a nice crunch and a bit of flair. With its fiery colors, this dish makes a beautiful conversation-stopping presentation.

I divided my recipe into seven small parts, each of which you prepare separately, then combine everything at the end. The trick here is to make sure you finish your prep before you cook—the actual cook time for the shrimp is only 5 minutes, so you'll have to move fast! To make the recipe easy to follow, I have paired the ingredients for each step with the instructions.

SHRIMP MARINADE

1 tablespoon sake

1 teaspoon sesame oil

¼ teaspoon salt

¼ teaspoon pepper

1 teaspoon cornstarch

14 ounces large shrimp, peeled and deveined, with tails on (you can use frozen 16/20 shrimp)

In a large bowl, combine the sake, oil, salt, pepper, and cornstarch. Add the shrimp and mix well. Cover and refrigerate for 15 to 20 minutes.

AROMATICS

2 tablespoons finely minced ginger

2 teaspoons finely minced garlic

Combine the ginger and garlic in a small bowl and set aside.

SWEET AND CHILI SAUCE

2 tablespoons tobanjan (Chinese chili paste)

5 tablespoons ketchup

1 tablespoon Japanese soy sauce

Combine all the ingredients in a small bowl, mix well, and set aside.

SAKE SAUCE

2 tablespoons sake

2 tablespoons sugar

¾ teaspoon salt

5 tablespoons water

Combine all the ingredients in a bowl, mix well, and set aside.

THICKENER

1 tablespoon cornstarch

1 tablespoon water

Mix the cornstarch and water together in a bowl and set aside. (Be sure to remix with a fork just before using.)

VINAIGRETTE

2 teaspoons rice wine vinegar

2 teaspoons sesame oil

Combine the ingredients in a bowl, mix well, and set aside.

(continued)

GARNISHES

2 scallions, both white and green parts, minced (see tip below)

2 sheets rice paper, halved (sold in supermarkets and Asian markets, made from rice flour)

Kosher salt

1 pint plus 3 tablespoons vegetable oil

To a large heavy-bottomed pan or deep fryer, add the 1 quart vegetable oil or enough oil to fill to 1 inch deep, and heat at 400°F until it begins to smoke. This may take up to 10 minutes.

Meanwhile, heat a large nonstick sauté pan and 1 tablespoon of the remaining vegetable oil over high heat for 1 minute, or until the oil begins to recede. Add the marinated shrimp in a single layer and slowly move around in the pan so they sear evenly on both sides but do not cook completely. Remove the shrimp from the pan and set aside in a bowl.

Decrease the heat to low. Add the remaining 2 tablespoons oil and the garlic and ginger aromatics. Continue to cook over low heat until the garlic just begins to brown, about 1 minute. Remove the pan from the heat, stir in the chili sauce, then add the sake sauce. Return the pan to the burner and increase the heat to high. Cook until the sauce comes to a boil, then return the shrimp to the pan and finish cooking, about 2 minutes longer. Stir in the cornstarch thickener until the sauce just begins to thicken. Remove the pan from the heat and mix in the vinaigrette and scallions.

By this time, the pan of oil should be just beginning to smoke. Turn off the heat and carefully drop in half a sheet of rice paper and immediately remove it using tongs. The rice paper will expand as soon as it makes contact with the hot oil, so it is important to move quickly. Gently place the puffed rice paper on a paper towel–lined plate and sprinkle with a pinch of kosher salt. Repeat with the remaining rice paper.

Transfer the shrimp to a large serving platter and set the puffed rice paper around the rim. Serve immediately.

TIP FOR MINCING SCALLIONS

Begin by slicing the scallions lengthwise into quarters, then bunch the pieces together and cut very thin. Finish by chopping the slices. This will save time by making the pieces smaller in the beginning.

Tofu Steak with Japanese Mushrooms

Serves 4

This is a very comforting, home-style dish, perfect for a blustery autumn day. Be sure to use only firm tofu for this recipe; softer varieties will fall apart during cooking. The trio of cultivated shiitake, enoki, and shimeji mushrooms is a classic combination in Japanese cooking, and it adds a nice woodsy and earthy flavor to this dish. You can use other kinds of mushrooms, too, if you'd like, everything from the humble button mushroom to fancier porcinis or chanterelles—whatever your budget allows.

BROTH

½ cup mirin

1½ cups Dashi (page 40)

¼ cup Japanese soy sauce

½ teaspoon salt

2 tablespoons cornstarch

2 tablespoons water

TOFU

2 tablespoons sesame oil

1 (19-ounce) package firm tofu, rinsed, patted dry, and cut into 4 long rectangles (approximately 1 by 2 by 3 inches)

¼ cup cornstarch

¼ cup thinly sliced celery

½ cup thinly sliced red onion

½ cup peeled and thinly sliced carrot

½ cup thinly sliced stemmed shiitake mushrooms

½ cup thinly sliced shimeji mushrooms

½ cup thinly sliced enoki mushrooms

1 scallion, both white and green parts, thinly sliced on an angle

2 obha leaves, halved and thinly sliced

To make the broth, combine the mirin, dashi, soy sauce, and salt in a small saucepan over medium heat. In a bowl, whisk together the cornstarch and water. Bring the broth just to a boil, then slowly whisk in the cornstarch mixture until the broth thickens slightly. Remove from the heat and set aside. (*Note:* The broth can be made up to 1 day in advance and stored in the refrigerator; reheat when ready to use.)

To prepare the tofu, heat an 11-inch nonstick sauté pan over medium heat. Add 1 tablespoon of the sesame oil. Lightly dredge the tofu pieces in the cornstarch and place in the hot pan. Cook until golden brown, 2½ to 3 minutes per side. Remove from the pan.

Using the same pan, add the remaining 1 tablespoon sesame oil, then the celery, red onion, carrot, shiitake mushrooms, shimeji mushrooms, and enoki mushrooms. Cook over high heat until the vegetables become soft, about 2 minutes, then add half the broth and cook for 30 seconds longer. Remove from the heat.

Set each piece of tofu in a shallow bowl and top with one-fourth of the cooked vegetables. Pour equal parts of the remaining broth into each bowl and garnish with the scallion and *obha* leaves.

Ingredients Glossary

Abura-Age
A thin, deep-fried sheet of tofu that opens up like pocket bread. Abura-age often comes marinated, so you need to pour boiling water on it before using to rinse off any excess oil. It can be stored in the freezer.

Daikon
A huge white radish that can grow to more than 1 foot long and 4 inches thick. Daikon is a fundamental ingredient in Japanese cooking and is eaten raw or cooked.

Enoki Mushrooms
Long, thin mushrooms that look like white-colored stalks of straw and grow in clusters. To use these cultivated mushrooms, cut off the thick base and separate the stalks by hand. Cook with both the stalks and the caps. They can stay in the refrigerator for up to a week.

Gobo
Burdock root, a brown-colored root that can grow a yard long, with a distinctive earthy flavor. Scrape off the skin with the back of a kitchen knife to reveal the white flesh, but be sure to place the cleaned gobo in water to remove bitterness and keep it from discoloring before you cook it.

Goma Paste
Japanese sesame paste that is quite similar to tahini. It is usually sold in a can much like its Middle Eastern cousin.

Hoisin Sauce
A tangy Chinese dipping sauce, sold in bottles at Asian food stores.

Ichimi Togarashi
Japanese dried red chili pepper flakes.

Japanese Curry Sauce Mix
Ready-made curry that is sold packaged as a paste in Japanese and Asian food stores. Comes in different degrees of heat.

Kaffir Lime Leaves
These fragrant and flavorful dark green leaves are a key ingredient in Thai cooking.

Kampyo
Long, dried strips of a type of squash. This ingredient is always sold dried.

Katsuobushi
Dried, smoked bonito that is shaved and used to prepare dashi (stock) or as a garnish for dishes. This ingredient is extremely important in Japanese cooking. Buy the thicker shavings for making stock, and the thinner, confetti-like shavings for garnishing.

Kimchi
A fundamental Korean ingredient with a history stretching back thousands of years. Produced by fermenting vegetables with seasonings, kimchi comes in many styles. The

most popular is made from cabbage (*baechu*) and is the one I call for in this book.

Kombu

A type of dried kelp that is another primary Japanese ingredient, often paired with katsuobushi to prepare dashi stock. It comes in sheets, from which you cut pieces as needed. It is stored at room temperature.

Lemongrass

An aromatic herb used extensively in Southeast Asian cooking. The stalk is often smashed to release flavor.

Lotus Root

Also called renkon, lotus root is a starchy vegetable with a crisp texture that is typically simmered or deep-fried. Peel the thick skin and soak in water before using.

Menma

Marinated, dried bamboo shoots; a popular condiment for ramen noodles.

Mentaiko

Spicy, preserved fish roe. Sometimes referred to as "spicy cod roe," but it's actually made from pollock fish eggs.

Mirin

A sweet liquid brewed from sticky rice that's an important flavoring agent in Japanese cooking. It has a low alcohol content but is used exclusively for cooking. Sometimes referred to as "sweet sake."

Miso (red, white, or brown)

Naturally preserved soybean paste. There are hundreds of varieties of this traditional Japanese ingredient, which is typically made from soybeans, salt, and rice or barley that ferment into a highly nutritious food, a process that can take months or even years. For the recipes in this book, stick to savory "red" rice miso, "white" rice miso, or "brown" rice miso.

Mitsuba

An aromatic trefoil herb that resembles flat parsley in appearance, but has a different taste. Sometimes referred to as "Japanese parsley." It can be substituted with watercress or daikon sprouts.

Naruto

A kind of Japanese fish cake with a signature spiral swirl that's used almost exclusively as a garnish for ramen.

Natto

Fermented soybeans with a distinct, nutty flavor and sticky texture. This traditional food is typically fermented for 24 hours to produce a strong taste reminiscent of a powerful cheese.

Negi

Often called "Japanese leek," these Welsh onions do indeed resemble large green leeks, with a long white cylinder that ends in roots.

Nori

Dried sheets of seaweed that resemble greenish brown paper. Their most common use is to wrap sushi rolls, but squares of nori are a typical garnish for certain ramen dishes. Nori is also available shredded like confetti, to garnish a host of dishes. Be sure to keep it dry.

Obha

An aromatic and flavorful herb that is sold as fresh, bright green leaves. The heart-shaped leaves have jagged edges.

Panko

A style of Japanese breadcrumb that is crispier and airier than typical breadcrumbs found in America.

Sake

Japan's classic alcoholic beverage, brewed from rice. Sometimes referred to as "rice wine," in fact it's produced in a manner more similar to beer. Much like wine, however, it is a sublime drink with many different varieties that reflect regionality, the maker, and the quality of ingredients.

Sakura Ebi

Tiny pink shrimp that are sold fresh or dried.

Sansho Pepper

Seedpods of the Japanese prickly ash ground into an aromatic pepper that produces a slight numbing effect on the tongue, much like Sichuan peppercorns. Sold already ground.

Shiitake Mushrooms

A cultivated, fragrant mushroom with a strong, distinct flavor that's used both fresh and dried. To use fresh shiitake mushrooms, cut off the stems, which aren't eaten, and cook with just the caps.

Shimeji Mushrooms

A cultivated mushroom that grows in a cluster of tan-colored stems and small caps. To use, cut off the base and separate the stems. Cook with both the stems and the caps.

Shungiku

The leafy greens of a type of chrysanthemum flower, this flavorful vegetable is often found in Japanese hot pot dishes.

Soy Sauce

Japanese soy sauce has a distinctly different flavor than Chinese and other Asian soy sauces, and should be used for the recipes in this book. We use three types of Japanese soy sauce for the recipes: *koikuchi*, which is the typical caramel-colored soy sauce; *usukuchi*, a lighter-colored soy sauce (but in fact saltier than *koikuchi*); and *shirojoyu*, "white" soy sauce, almost clear-colored.

Sunchang Kochujang

A ready-made spicy miso bean sauce from Korea used to add heat to certain dishes.

Tobanjan

A bright red Chinese chili paste that's used in Japanese cooking, especially ramen.

Tofu

Japanese tofu, or soybean curd, comes in different degrees of firmness. Some of the recipes call for firm tofu, while others call for "silken" or soft tofu. Both types are clearly marked on their packaging.

Tonkatsu Sauce

A tangy, ready-made sauce that is the Japanese equivalent of Worcestershire sauce and is as common in Japan as ketchup is in America.

Umeboshi

Often referred to as "Japanese pickled plum," it is a type of Japanese apricot that is salted and pickled. Red in color, it has a sour and salty taste that adds depth to recipes.

Wakame

Seaweed that comes dried or salted and is reconstituted by soaking in hot water.

Wasabi

Real wasabi is a root that has a spicy taste like hot mustard. Often called "Japanese horseradish," it's also sold as a powder or ready-to-use paste, which is a close approximation to the real thing and is used extensively in home and restaurant cooking.

Yamaimo

A yam with spiky, tan-colored skin and white flesh, shaped like a baton. Peel the skin and grate the flesh, which becomes gooey but has a delicate flavor.

Yuzu

A tart Japanese citrus whose aromatic zest is used as a garnish and whose juice is used as a seasoning. If not available fresh, you can buy the dried peel or a small bottle of the juice.

Yuzu Pepper (Yuzu Kosho)

A hot, spicy condiment that's a combination of yuzu citrus zest and chile peppers.

Zarsai

Salty and pungent Chinese pickles, usually comprised of radishes or a kind of bok choy.

Resources

You can find Japanese ingredients in Asian food stores across the country, including these Japanese markets:

Daido
White Plains, New York;
Fort Lee, New Jersey; and
Houston, Texas
www.daidomarket.com

**Daruma Japanese
Market**
Bethesda, Maryland
www.darumajapanmarket
.com

Ebisu Supermarket
Fountain Valley, California
www.ocebisu.com

JAS Mart
New York, New York
(212) 866-4780

Katagiri
New York, New York
www.katagiri.com

Kotobukiya
Cambridge,
Massachussetts
www.kotobukiyamarket
.com

Maido
Narbeth, Pennsylvania
www.maidookini.com

Marukai
throughout California and
Hawaii
www.marukai.com

Mitsuwa
throughout California,
Illinois, and New Jersey
www.mitsuwa.com/
english

Naniwa Foods
McLean, VA
(703) 893-7209

Nijiya Market
Hartsdale, New York
and multiple locations in
California
www.nijiya.com

One World Market
Novi, Michigan
(248) 374-0844

**Pacific Mercantile
Company**
Denver, Colorado
www.pacificeastwest.com

Shop Minoya
Plano, Texas
(972) 769-8346

Sunrise Mart
New York, New York
(212) 598-3040

Tensuke Market
Elk Grove Village, Illinois
www.tensuke.us

Tensuke Market
Columbus, Ohio
www.tensukemarket.com

Tokyo Japanese Store
Pittsburgh, Pennsylvania
www.tokyostorepgh.com

Tokyo Fish Market
Albany, California
(510) 524-7243

Uwajimaya
Seattle, Washington;
Bellevue, Washington; and
Beaverton, Oregon
www.uwajimaya.com

Yamasho, Inc. (wholesale)
Elk Grove Village, Illinois
www.yamashoinc.com

Index

Shio Base

Makes 5 cups

Use this base for Shio Ramen (page 22) and other recipes. You want this broth to be light colored, which is why I use "white" soy sauce, an almost clear liquid, rather than typical caramel-hued soy sauce.

1 piece kombu, wiped with a damp cloth

1 cup shirojoyu (white soy sauce)

4 cups water

¾ cup kosher or sea salt

1½ cups katsuobushi (dried bonito flakes)

Combine all the ingredients in a saucepan. Place over high heat and bring to a boil, then reduce the heat and simmer for 10 minutes. Strain through a fine-mesh sieve.

To make *shio* broth, combine 2 cups Ramen Chicken Stock (page 10) with 3 ounces (¼ cup plus 2 tablespoons) *shio* base.

Shoyu Base

Makes 4½ cups

This is the base for Shoyu Ramen (page 24) and other ramen recipes in this section.

1 piece kombu, wiped with a damp cloth

1½ cups shirojoyu (white soy sauce)

2 cups water

1 tablespoon plus ½ teaspoon kosher or sea salt

1 cup Japanese soy sauce

1½ cups katsuobushi (dried bonito flakes)

Combine all the ingredients in a saucepan. Place over high heat and bring to a boil, then reduce the heat and simmer for 10 minutes. Strain through a fine-mesh sieve.

To make shoyu broth, combine 2 cups Ramen Chicken Stock (page 10) with 3 ounces (¼ cup plus 2 tablespoons) shoyu base.

Chiyan-Pon-Men

Serves 4

I still remember the first time I tasted these crispy, Chinese-style noodles, on a high school trip to the southern Japanese port city of Nagasaki. This ramen dish is a hallmark of that part of the country, especially when combined with seafood—the seafood in Nagasaki is unbelievably good. This area is also geographically close to China and Korea, and is influenced by their cultures. Nagasaki, in fact, has the oldest Chinatown in Japan, established in the 1600s. You can try other seafood combinations in this recipe, too. Fish also works great with fried ramen noodles.

¼ cup dried wood ear mushrooms

1 cup hot water

¼ cup sesame oil

8 shrimp, peeled and deveined, with tails on

4 pieces squid, cleaned and cut into ¼-inch-thick rings

20 bay scallops (about 4 ounces)

16 pea pods, stemmed

4 cups chopped napa cabbage

1 cup stemmed enoki mushrooms

½ cup sliced canned water chestnuts

½ cup peeled and thinly sliced carrots

1 cup chopped baby bok choy

¼ cup Shio Base (page 11)

2 cups Ramen Chicken Stock (page 10)

2 tablespoons rice vinegar

¼ cup Japanese soy sauce

4 teaspoons sugar

2 tablespoons cornstarch

2 tablespoons cold water

Dash of hot chili oil

Pinch of ground pepper

6 ounces age-men (ready-made fried ramen noodles, available in Asian food stores)

4 teaspoons hot mustard

In a small bowl, cover the wood ear mushrooms with the hot water and let sit for 10 minutes. Drain the liquid and thinly slice the mushrooms. Set aside.

Heat 2 tablespoons of the sesame oil in a very large sauté pan or wide pot placed over high heat. Add the shrimp and cook for 1 minute, then add the squid and scallops. Cook for an additional minute, or until all the seafood is seared on each side but not necessarily cooked through. Remove the seafood from the pan and set aside.

Add the remaining 2 tablespoons sesame oil to the same pan and return it to high heat. Add the pea pods, napa cabbage, enoki and wood ear mushrooms, water chestnuts, carrots, and bok choy. Cook for 2 minutes, stirring frequently.

Meanwhile, combine the *Shio* Base and chicken stock in a small pot over high heat. Bring the liquid to a boil, then add it to the sautéed vegetables. Add in the seafood, followed by the vinegar, soy sauce, and sugar.

In a small bowl, combine the cornstarch and water. Add it to the boiling liquid and cook for an additional minute. Season to taste with the chili oil and ground pepper.

Divide the fried noodles among 4 plates and place 1 teaspoon of hot mustard on the side of each plate. Top the noodles with one-fourth of the seafood and vegetable mixture. Mix well before eating.

Chilled Crab and Shrimp Ramen Salad with Chukka-Soba Dressing

Serves 4

When these noodles appear on restaurant menus in Japan, it heralds just one thing: the arrival of summer. This ramen is a classic warm-weather dish, popular from June until September. *Chukka* means "Chinese," a reference to the origins of ramen noodles. And it's not just a restaurant dish—when I was growing up, my mother loved to prepare this for our family.

CHUKKA-SOBA DRESSING

¼ cup Japanese soy sauce

¼ cup rice vinegar

¼ cup sake

1 tablespoon sesame oil

2 tablespoons lemon juice

½ teaspoon grated ginger

¼ cup sugar

Dash of hot chili oil

EGG OMELET

2 eggs

1 tablespoon half-and-half

2 teaspoons sugar

¼ teaspoon Japanese soy sauce

Pinch of kosher salt

1 teaspoon vegetable oil

SHRIMP

8 large shrimp, peeled and deveined, with tails off

8 (3-inch) bamboo skewers

2 tablespoons kosher salt

ASSEMBLY

2 tablespoons dried wakame

1 cup hot water

4 (7-ounce) pieces frozen ramen noodles

2 ounces crabmeat

2 cups iceberg lettuce, thinly sliced

12 grape tomatoes, halved

½ cup thinly sliced ham

1 cup thinly sliced cucumber sticks

½ cup thinly sliced carrot sticks

¼ cup thinly sliced pickled ginger

Pinch of black sesame seeds

½ cup shredded nori

To make the dressing, whisk together all ingredients until well combined. Set aside.

To make the omelet, whisk the eggs, half-and-half, sugar, soy sauce, and salt together in a bowl. Place a nonstick sauté pan over medium-high heat. Pour ½ teaspoon of the vegetable oil into the pan and coat evenly using a paper towel; discard the excess oil. Once the oil is hot, pour half the egg mixture into the pan in a thin layer and cook until almost dry, about 2 minutes, then flip with a flat-bottomed spatula and cook for an additional 2 minutes. Remove from the pan and set on a plate to cool. Repeat with the

(continued)

remaining egg mixture and oil to make the second omelet. Once cool, thinly slice the omelets. Refrigerate until ready to serve.

To prepare the shrimp, butterfly the shrimp as follows: With a paring knife, make a cut along the underside of the shrimp, being careful not to cut through them entirely (the shrimp should lie flat but still remain in one piece). Press down lightly on the shrimp so they lie flat, then thread one shrimp onto each skewer.

Add the salt to a large pot of water and bring to a simmer. While the water is simmering, prepare an ice bath. Add the shrimp to the simmering water and cook until they are cooked through, about 90 seconds (they turn pink and are no longer translucent). Transfer the shrimp to the ice bath. Once they're cool, drain, pat dry, and season with a pinch of salt.

To assemble the dish, in a bowl, cover the wakame with the hot water and let sit for 10 minutes. Drain well and set aside.

Prepare an ice bath and place a large pot of water over high heat to bring to boil. Add the noodles and cook following the package instructions. Remove the noodles from the water and submerge in the ice bath. Drain well.

Divide the noodles among 4 plates and top each with 2 tablespoons of the dressing. Place one-fourth each of the crabmeat, lettuce, tomatoes, ham, cucumber, carrots, shrimp, omelet, and wakame in small piles on the noodles to form a circle. Sprinkle the pickled ginger over the salad, then drizzle another 2 tablespoons of dressing over the top. Garnish with the black sesame seeds and shredded nori.

Braised Ramen with Pork and Zarsai

Serves 2

When I was the chef of Tribute, in Farmington Hills, Michigan, I was always hungry by the time my restaurant closed. (Little known fact: chefs never have time to eat!) So I'd usually stop by a local Chinese place on the way home, which is where I discovered this delicious dish. The chef there introduced me to cooking with *zarsai*, which are salty and pungent Chinese pickles, usually radishes or a kind of bok choy. Eaten on their own, they make you thirst for a beer, but cooked, they mellow and add great flavor to a dish. I love serving these noodles in a clay pot, or *donabe*. It gives it a warm and comforting touch, especially in wintertime.

MARINATED PORK

1 cup thinly sliced pork loin

1 tablespoon sake

1 tablespoon Japanese soy sauce

SHOYU BROTH

2 cups Ramen Chicken Stock (page 10)

3 fluid ounces Shoyu Base (page 10)

ASSEMBLY

1 tablespoon vegetable oil

1 teaspoon minced garlic

⅓ cup thinly sliced bamboo shoots

½ cup thinly sliced green bell pepper

½ cup zarsai (Chinese pickled vegetables)

3 tablespoons cornstarch

3 tablespoons cold water

2 (7-ounce) pieces frozen ramen noodles

½ cup thinly sliced scallions, white part only

Hot chili oil

To make the pork, combine the pork, sake, and soy sauce in a bowl and mix well. Cover and refrigerate for 20 minutes.

To make the broth, combine the chicken stock and Shoyu Base in a saucepan over light heat. Bring to a boil, then reduce the heat to low and cover to keep warm.

To prepare the dish, place a large sauté pan over high heat. Add the vegetable oil and garlic. Cook until the garlic is fragrant and just beginning to turn golden, about 30 seconds, then mix in the marinated pork and cook, stirring, for 1 minute. Stir in the bamboo shoots, bell pepper, and *zarsai* and cook for 1 to 2 minutes, or until the vegetables become soft. Pour the broth into the pan and bring the liquid to a boil.

In a small bowl, whisk together the cornstarch and water. Add the mixture to the broth and decrease the heat to low. Simmer the broth for 1 minute, or until it thickens slightly. Turn off the heat and set aside.

Bring a pot of water to a boil. Cook the ramen noodles for just 30 seconds, or until the noodles become loose but are not completely cooked through. Drain the noodles and divide them between 2 *donabe*, and place the *donabe* on the stove top. Pour half the broth into each *donabe* and turn the heat to medium-high. Top each with half the pork and vegetables. Once the liquid comes to a boil, garnish each with half the scallions and a dash of chili oil. Cover the *donabe* and turn off the heat. Carefully set them on plates and serve hot.

Chilled Ramen with Chicken and Banbanji Sauce

Serves 4

Banbanji is a Chinese-inspired spicy sesame sauce that pairs wonderfully with chilled ramen noodles, a perfect summertime dish. Instead of grilling the chicken in this recipe, which is typical for cold dishes, you sear the skin side, then steam in sake. This results in crispy skin but incredibly moist chicken with a hint of sake flavor. With this technique, the chicken will always remain juicy and tender, even after you cool it. You can store the *banbanji* sauce in your refrigerator or freezer and use it over and over.

SAKE-STEAMED CHICKEN

1 boneless chicken breast with skin, cleaned and trimmed

1 boneless chicken thigh with skin, cleaned and trimmed

Pinch each of kosher salt and pepper

2 tablespoons vegetable oil

¼ cup sake

BANBANJI SAUCE

¼ cup tahini (sesame paste)

2 tablespoons Japanese soy sauce

2 teaspoons tobanjan (Chinese chili paste)

4 teaspoons sugar

1 tablespoon rice vinegar

4 teaspoons sesame oil

2 teaspoons minced ginger

1 tablespoon sake

Dash of hot chili oil

1 scallion, both white and green parts, minced

ASSEMBLY

¼ cup thinly sliced scallion, both white and green parts

4 (7-ounce) pieces frozen ramen noodles

1 cup thinly sliced cucumber sticks
    (2 inches long by ¼ inch wide)

¾ cup Chukka-Soba Dressing (page 15), chilled

To cook the chicken, begin by seasoning both sides of the breast and thigh with salt and pepper. Pour the oil into a pot (the pot should be just large enough for the chicken to lie flat on the bottom without a lot of extra room) and set it over high heat. When the oil just begins to smoke, add the chicken skin side down. Cook the chicken until the skin turns golden brown and the meat is halfway cooked through, about 6 minutes. Turn the chicken over in the pan and drain the excess oil. Add the sake and cover the pan with a tight-fitting lid. Reduce the heat to low and let the chicken cook for another 5 minutes, then turn off the heat and let it sit in the pot for a few minutes to finish cooking. Transfer the chicken to a plate and refrigerate until cool.

While the chicken is cooling, **make the *banbanji* sauce.** In a bowl, combine all the ingredients; mix well. Set aside.

To assemble the dish, soak the scallion slices in cold water for 10 minutes, then drain well. Once the chicken has cooled, slice it into ¼-inch-thick pieces.

Place a large pot of water over high heat and bring to a boil. Cook the noodles, following package instructions. Drain and rinse well under cold running water.

Divide the noodles among 4 bowls. Top each bowl of noodles with one-quarter of the chicken and cucumber, then drizzle 3 tablespoons of the Chukka-Soba Dressing over each bowl followed by 1½ tablespoons of the *banbanji* sauce. Garnish with the scallions.

Miso Ramen

Serves 4

This ramen is a wintertime standard in Japan, and no wonder: it hails from the city of Sapporo in the far northern island of Hokkaido (home of the eponymous beer), a part of the country that's very frigid and snowy in the winter. The hearty pork and miso-flavored broth in this dish is the perfect warm-up for even the chilliest day. Miso ramen is a relative newcomer to the noodle scene, becoming popular only since the mid-sixties. But corn, a surprising ingredient for a Japanese dish, has been grown in Hokkaido since the nineteenth century.

MISO BASE

2 tablespoons sesame oil

½ cup minced onion

2 tablespoons grated ginger

¼ cup minced garlic

1 cup ground pork (about 8 ounces)

½ cup shiro miso (white miso)

¼ cup ada miso (red miso)

¼ cup ground sesame seeds

5 tablespoons hoisin sauce

1 tablespoon tobanjan (Chinese chili paste)

3 tablespoons Japanese soy sauce

MISO RAMEN

8 cups Ramen Chicken Stock (page 10)

2 tablespoons vegetable oil

8 cups bean sprouts

⅔ cup garlic chives, cut into 1-inch lengths

4 (7-ounce) pieces frozen ramen noodles

½ cup drained canned sweet corn

4 teaspoons ground sesame seeds

Pinch of sansho pepper (Japanese pepper seedpods)

2 scallions, both white and green parts, thinly sliced on an angle

To make the miso base, combine the sesame oil, onion, ginger, and garlic in a small saucepan over medium-low heat. Cook, stirring often, for 6 minutes, or until the ingredients are soft and fragrant. Mix in the ground pork and increase the heat to medium. Cook for an additional 6 to 7 minutes, or until the pork is completely cooked through.

Stir in both misos, the sesame seeds, hoisin sauce, *tobanjan*, and soy sauce, and bring to a boil. Turn off the heat and set aside. Leftover miso base will keep refrigerated for up to 1 week or frozen for up to 2 months.

To make the ramen, combine the ramen chicken stock and 1¾ cups of the miso base in a pot set over high heat to make the miso broth. Bring to a boil, then reduce the heat to low and cover to keep warm. Place another large pot over high heat and bring to a boil.

Heat the vegetable oil in a large, wide-bottomed pot over high heat. Add the bean sprouts and garlic chives and cook for 1 minute, stirring often. Add the miso broth and bring to a boil. Cook for 1 minute, then turn off the heat.

Add the ramen noodles to the boiling water and cook, following package instructions. Drain well and divide among 4 bowls. Top each with one-fourth of the broth and vegetables. Garnish each bowl with 2 tablespoons of the corn kernels, 1 teaspoon of the ground sesame seeds, the sansho pepper, and one-fourth of the sliced scallions. Serve hot.

Mushroom Ramen

Serves 4

My love affair with mushrooms started when I was a kid, when I would go wild-mushroom hunting with my father in the forests that surrounded my hometown of Mito. I still love their earthy, nutty taste, and the different textures found in different varieties. In fact, when you dine at my restaurant, you'll see I use them in everything from appetizers to main courses. Mushroom ramen isn't a dish you'll typically see in a Japanese ramen shop, but I think the two ingredients work perfectly, especially accented with *shungiku*, which are tangy chrysanthemum leaves.

SHIO BROTH

8 cups Ramen Chicken Stock (page 10)

1½ cups Shio Base (page 11)

MUSHROOM RAMEN

2 tablespoons sesame oil

1 cup peeled and thinly sliced gobo (burdock root; can substitute with salsify)

1 cup drained canned straw mushrooms

10 shiitake mushrooms, stemmed and sliced into ¼-inch-thick pieces

2 cups trimmed shimeji mushrooms

1 cup stemmed enoki mushrooms

1 tablespoon minced garlic

1⅓ cups small tofu cubes (about 7 ounces, cut into ½ inch squares)

½ cup chopped scallions, both white and green parts

20 sprigs shungiku, cut into thirds

¼ cup cornstarch

¼ cup cold water

4 (7-ounce) pieces frozen ramen noodles

4 teaspoons garlic chips (page 106)

To make the broth, combine the chicken stock and *Shio* Base in a pot placed over high heat. Bring to a boil, then reduce the heat to low and cover to keep warm.

To make the ramen, in a very large sauté pan or wide-bottomed pot, heat the sesame oil over medium heat. Add the gobo and cook until caramelized on all sides, about 3 minutes. Add all the mushrooms and the garlic and increase the heat to high. Cook for another 3 minutes, stirring often, then add the *shio* broth and tofu.

Once the liquid comes to a boil, add the scallions and *shungiku*. Cook for 1 minute. In a small bowl, whisk together the cornstarch and cold water and add to the boiling broth. Cook for 1 minute longer, then decrease the heat to low.

Place a large pot of water over high heat and bring to a boil. Add the ramen noodles and cook, following package instructions. Drain well and divide among 4 bowls. Top each with the one-fourth of the broth and vegetables, and garnish with 1 teaspoon of the garlic chips.

Seaweed, Avocado, and Hearts of Palm Noodle Salad

Serves 4

Call this my Japanese-inspired take on cobb salad, except that it's all vegetarian. It's a perfect dish for summertime eating. I love sweet and crispy hearts of palm, which are native to Latin America. Try to buy them fresh, if possible, but canned works fine, too. The umeboshi-yuzu vinaigrette lends the vegetables an irresistible tangy and citrusy flavor. Ramen noodles served chilled are springy, chewy, and absolutely delicious.

UMEBOSHI-YUZU VINAIGRETTE

¼ cup Japanese soy sauce

¼ cup yuzu juice (can substitute with lemon juice)

2 teaspoons lemon juice

2 umeboshi (pickled Japanese apricots), pitted and chopped

¼ cup sake

1 tablespoon sesame oil

¼ cup sugar

½ teaspoon grated ginger

¼ teaspoon salt

Dash of hot chili oil

1½ tablespoons dried wakame

1 cup hot water

½ English cucumber

4 (7-ounce) pieces frozen ramen noodles

2 cups diced romaine lettuce

12 cherry tomatoes, quartered

1 avocado, cored and sliced into ¼-inch-thick pieces

½ cup thinly sliced carrots

2 pieces hearts of palm, sliced into ¼-inch-thick pieces on an angle (about 16 pieces)

4 obha leaves, thinly sliced

2 teaspoons sesame seeds

To make the vinaigrette, combine all the ingredients in a bowl and whisk until well combined. Set aside.

To make the salad, in a small bowl, cover the wakame with the hot water and let sit for 10 minutes. Drain well and set aside.

Prepare the English cucumber by peeling the skin to resemble stripes, then cut it in half lengthwise and scoop out the seeds. Slice the cucumber halves into ¼-inch-thick pieces on an angle.

Place a large pot of water over high heat and bring to a boil. Add the noodles and cook, following package instructions. Rinse under cold running water until the noodles are chilled. Drain well and divide among 4 plates.

To assemble the salad, top each pile of noodles with the lettuce, cucumber, cherry tomatoes, avocado, carrots, hearts of palm, and wakame. Garnish with the *obha* leaves and sesame seeds, then drizzle the dressing over each plate.

Shio Ramen

Serves 4

Like Miso Ramen (page 19), Shio Ramen hails from the northern Japanese city of Sapporo, and is a perfect antidote to a frigid winter day. *Shio* means "salt" in Japanese, and indeed, the clear broth has an appealing sea-salt flavor. These noodles are a relatively late addition to the ramen lineup, but they're now popular across Japan. This is the classic recipe, which is loaded with fresh vegetables.

8 pea pods, trimmed

1 tablespoon dried wakame

1 cup hot water

8 cups Ramen Chicken Stock (page 10)

1½ cups Shio Base (page 11)

¼ cup vegetable oil

2 tablespoons minced garlic

½ cup plus 2 tablespoons ground pork

2 tablespoons hoisin sauce

1 teaspoon tobanjan (Chinese chili paste)

½ cup sliced onion

½ cup peeled and thinly sliced carrots (sliced on an angle)

8 shiitake mushrooms, stems removed and cut into ¼-inch-thick slices

½ green cabbage, cored and cut into bite-size pieces

4 cups bean sprouts, rinsed well

4 (7-ounce) pieces frozen ramen noodles

1 tablespoon ground sesame seeds

2 scallions, both white and green parts, thinly sliced on an angle

Dash of hot chili oil

Prepare an ice bath and place a large pot of water over high heat. When the water comes to a boil, add the pea pods and cook for 1 minute. Remove the pea pods from the water and submerge in the ice bath. Once cool, drain the pea pods and cut in half. Set aside. Keep the boiling water to cook the noodles in later.

In a bowl, cover the wakame with the hot water and let sit for 10 minutes. Drain well and set aside.

Combine the chicken stock and *Shio* Base in a pot and place over high heat to make the *shio* broth. Bring just to a boil, then reduce the heat to low and cover to keep warm.

Heat 2 tablespoons of the vegetable oil in a very large sauté pan or wide-bottomed pot over high heat. Once hot, add the garlic and cook for 30 seconds, stirring constantly, but be careful not to let the garlic burn. Mix in the ground pork and cook for 2 minutes. Add the hoisin sauce and *tobanjan* and continue cooking, stirring constantly with a wooden spoon to break up the pork into small pieces. Cook for 5 minutes, then remove the pork from the pan and set aside.

Add the remaining 2 tablespoons vegetable oil to the pan and return it to high heat. Add the onions, carrots, mushrooms, cabbage, and pea pods. Cook until the vegetables begin to soften, stirring often, about 3 minutes. Mix in the bean sprouts and reserved pork. Cook for 1 minute, then pour the heated *shio* broth into the pan. Bring the liquid to a boil, then reduce the heat to low.

Cook the ramen noodles in the reserved boiling water according to package instructions. Drain well and divide among 4 bowls. Top each bowl with one-fourth of the broth, vegetables, and pork, and garnish with the ground sesame seeds, reserved wakame, scallions, and hot chili oil to taste.

Spicy Oil with Chilled Ramen

Serves 4

This is a simple recipe that combines wonderful, distinct flavors. Japanese black vinegar, also referred to as aged rice vinegar, is an artisanal product naturally brewed from rice with a complexity akin to a fine balsamic vinegar. The hot oil adds terrific flavor and great aroma, a perfect accent to this dish—but be very careful heating the oil.

SPICY MISO SAUCE

2 tablespoons sunchang kochujang (Korean miso sauce)

2 tablespoons nam pla (fish sauce)

¼ cup kurosu (aged rice vinegar; or substitute with balsamic vinegar)

2 tablespoons lime juice

ASSEMBLY

4 cups bean sprouts

4 (7-ounce) pieces frozen ramen noodles

1 cup thinly sliced scallions, both white and green parts

16 sprigs cilantro

2 tablespoons thinly sliced ginger

½ cup dried sakura ebi (Japanese shrimp)

2 tablespoons chili threads (available in Japanese and Asian stores)

4 teaspoons spicy mustard (Asian hot mustard)

SPICY OIL

6 tablespoons sesame oil

1½ teaspoons hot chili oil

To make the sauce, combine all the ingredients in a bowl and whisk until well combined. Set aside.

To assemble the dish, bring a large pot of water to boil over high heat. Add the bean sprouts and cook for 10 seconds. Remove the sprouts from the water (but keep the pot of hot water) and refrigerate until ready to serve.

Return the water to a boil, add the noodles, and cook, following package instructions. Rinse the noodles under cold running water until they are cool, then drain well. Divide the noodles among 4 plates, arranging the noodles in a tall, compact pile.

Top each plate of noodles with one-fourth of the bean sprouts, scallions, cilantro, ginger, *sakura ebi*, and chili threads. Add 1 teaspoon spicy mustard on the side of each plate and pour 2 tablespoons of the sauce over the top of the noodles.

To make the oil, combine the sesame oil and hot chili oil in a small bowl. Heat a sauté pan over high heat until very hot, then add the oil mixture, which will make "popping" sounds. Be careful not to get splattered by the hot oil. Remove the pan from the heat once the popping subsides and top each plate with 2 teaspoons of the oil, again being very careful. Mix well before eating.

Tantanmen

Serves 4

Spice alert: this ramen is guaranteed to make you sweat. These snappy noodles are very popular in Japan, even in the summer—some people, I guess, don't find our sultry and humid hot season sticky enough! I, for one, prefer this ramen in the winter, because its rich pork and miso broth is warm and comforting.

2 teaspoons tobanjan (Chinese chili paste)

2 tablespoons hoisin sauce

2 tablespoons Japanese soy sauce

2 teaspoons sugar

4 cups Ramen Chicken Stock (page 10)

2 cups Miso Base (page 19)

2 tablespoons sesame oil

2 tablespoons minced garlic

12 ounces ground pork

4 (7-ounce) pieces frozen ramen noodles

2 pieces baby bok choy, halved

2 scallions, both white and green parts, thinly sliced on an angle

Mix together the *tobanjan*, hoisin sauce, soy sauce, and sugar in a bowl and set aside.

Combine the chicken stock and Miso Base in a pot placed over high heat to make the miso broth. Bring to a boil, then reduce the heat to low and cover to keep warm. In addition, place another large pot of water over high heat and bring to a boil.

Heat the sesame oil in a large sauté pan placed over high heat. Add the garlic and cook for 10 seconds, then mix in the ground pork. After 1 minute, add the reserved sauce mixture and cook, stirring constantly to break up the pork, for 2 minutes longer, or until the pork is cooked through. Set aside.

Add the noodles and bok choy to the boiling water and cook for 1 minute. Drain the liquid and set aside the bok choy. Divide the noodles among 4 bowls and top each with 2 cups of miso broth. Divide the pork among the bowls and garnish each with the bok choy and scallions.

Tenshinmen

Serves 4

This is a classic ramen dish that was one of my favorites when I was growing up, but today it's not as popular as it used to be in Japan. That's a shame, because there's so much to love about this dish, especially the play between the sweetness of the crab and the crunchiness of the water chestnuts, and the dramatic presentation of a big chunk of omelet sitting atop the noodles. This dish is finished with two kinds of broth, one to serve as the soup, the other to add a bit of sheen as a glaze. I hope you love this ramen as much as I do.

SHOYU BROTH

5½ cups Ramen Chicken Stock (page 10)

1 cup Shoyu Base (page 11)

SHOYU GLAZE

1 tablespoon cornstarch

1 tablespoon water

OMELETS

10 eggs

12 ounces crabs legs, removed from the shell and roughly shredded (can substitute imitation crabmeat)

¼ cup garlic chives, cut into 1-inch pieces

½ cup spring peas (fresh or frozen)

½ cup diced water chestnuts

2 tablespoons Japanese soy sauce

Pinch each of salt and pepper

¼ cup vegetable oil

4 (7-ounce) pieces frozen ramen noodles

To make the broth, combine the chicken stock and Shoyu Base in a pot and place over high heat. Bring just to a boil, then decrease the heat to low and cover to keep warm. Place another large pot of water over high heat and bring to a boil.

To make the glaze, pour 1 cup of the shoyu broth into a small pot over high heat, and bring it to a boil. In a small bowl, whisk together the cornstarch and water and stir it into the boiling broth. Decrease the heat to medium and simmer for 5 minutes, then decrease the heat to low and cover to keep warm.

To prepare the omelets, beat the eggs in a large bowl. Mix in the crab, garlic chives, green peas, water chestnuts, soy sauce, and ½ cup of the shoyu broth, and season with the salt and pepper.

Place a 9-inch nonstick sauté pan over high heat and add 1 tablespoon of the vegetable oil. Once the oil is hot, pour in one-fourth of the egg mixture. Cook for 2 to 3 minutes over high heat, lightly stirring the center of the omelet with a large spoon, until most of the liquid has solidified. Reduce the heat to low and cook for 1 minute longer, then place a plate over the top of the pan, and flip the pan over in one fluid motion to invert the omelet onto the plate. Gently slide the omelet back into the pan with the cooked side up. Cook for 1 minute longer over low heat, then slide the omelet from the pan onto a plate. The omelet should be thick and golden brown on one side. Repeat with the remaining oil and egg mixture to make 3 more omelets.

Cook the noodles in the boiling water, following package instructions. Drain well and divide among 4 bowls. Top each with an omelet, 1¼ cups shoyu broth, and ¼ cup shoyu glaze. Serve hot.

Tsukemen Ramen

Serves 4

Tsukumen means, literally, "dipping ramen," and it's a dish that's taken Japan by storm. When I was growing up, we didn't eat ramen this way, but now you can find this dish offered in shops across the country. It's not hard to understand why—eating ramen in this deconstructed way gives you a chance to enjoy the noodle and each of the garnishes on its own, dipped in the flavorful broth. This dish is also a delicious play between cold ramen and hot broth. Think of it as noodle nouvelle cuisine! *Naruto* has a signature spiral swirl, and interestingly enough, it's an ingredient used almost exclusively for ramen (and on rare occasions, udon).

BROTH

1 cup plus 1 tablespoon Shoyu Base (page 11)

4 cups Ramen Chicken Stock (page 10)

2 tablespoons sugar

2 tablespoons rice vinegar

1 tablespoon sesame oil

RAMEN

4 (7-ounce) pieces frozen ramen noodles

2 tablespoons dried wakame

2 cups hot water

8 pieces Braised Pork Belly (page 138)

½ cup sliced scallions, both white and green parts

8 slices naruto (fish cake)

½ cup menma (marinated bamboo shoots)

To make the broth, combine all the ingredients in a pot and place over high heat. Bring the liquid to a boil, then reduce the heat to low and cover to keep warm.

To make the ramen, place a large pot of water over high heat and bring to a boil. Add the noodles and cook, following package instructions. Rinse the noodles well under cold running water until they are chilled. Drain and divide among 4 plates.

In a small bowl, cover the wakame with the hot water and let sit for 10 minutes. Drain well.

To serve, arrange small piles of the wakame, pork belly, scallions, *naruto*, and bamboo shoots in a circle on top of the noodles. Divide the hot broth among 4 small bowls and serve on the side. Dip the noodles and garnishes into the broth to eat.

Yakisoba

Serves 4

Yakisoba is an extremely popular casual dish in Japan, especially with kids. During the country's annual summer festivals you can always find yakisoba stands crowded next to shrines and temples, ready to feed hungry visitors. Traditionally, this dish is prepared with pork loin or pork belly, but I think it tastes really wonderful with beef. Also, I prefer to use dried ramen noodles rather than frozen because they stay al dente when added to the stir-fry.

2 (3-ounce) pieces dried ramen noodles

3 tablespoons vegetable oil

6 ounces thinly sliced beef rib eye

1 cup thinly sliced onions

½ cup peeled and thinly sliced carrots

8 shiitake mushrooms, stemmed and thinly sliced

½ cup stemmed enoki mushrooms

4 scallions, both white and green parts, thinly sliced on an angle

¼ cabbage, cored and thinly sliced

4 cups bean sprouts

½ cup tonkatsu sauce (semisweet)

1 tablespoon ketchup

1 tablespoon Japanese soy sauce

2 tablespoons beni shoga (red pickled ginger)

2 tablespoons finely shaved katsuobushi (dried bonito flakes)

Place a large pot of water over high heat and bring to a boil. Add the noodles and cook, following package instructions. Rinse under cold running water. Once chilled, drain well and set aside.

While the noodles are cooking, heat 2 tablespoons of the vegetable oil in a large sauté pan placed over high heat. When the oil just begins to smoke, stir in the beef and cook for 1 minute, stirring often. Remove the beef from the pan and place it on a plate. Set aside.

Return the pan with the oil still in it to high heat and add the remaining 1 tablespoon oil. Add the onions, carrots, both mushrooms, scallions, and cabbage. Cook for 3 to 4 minutes, stirring often, until the vegetables just begin to soften. Add the bean sprouts, cooked noodles, and beef, and cook for 1 minute longer, until all the ingredients are heated through.

Stir in the tonkatsu sauce, ketchup, and soy sauce. Cook for 1 to 2 minutes for the sauce to thicken, stirring often. Remove the pan from the heat and divide the noodles, vegetables, and beef among 4 plates. Garnish each one with the beni shoga and bonito flakes.

CHAPTER TWO | Soba

SOBA

SOBA is another beloved noodle in Japan, but one that has two lives: it's a down-home soul food, like ramen, but it also has a more elegant side, elevated to a high art by celebrated soba chefs who prepare it from scratch. I love them both ways.

Soba noodles are made from buckwheat flour and first appeared in Japan around the seventeenth century, when shops and street vendors started hawking them. They began as a humble food, sustenance for priests, laborers, and the lower classes. But before long, aristocrats and lords discovered these delicious noodles, and elegant soba restaurants opened to serve them. America even got an early taste of soba, when it was featured in the 1893 World's Fair in my adopted hometown of Chicago!

Soba is the signature noodle of the northeastern region around Tokyo, where I was born. In fact, I grew up next to a soba restaurant owned by a classmate's family, and I spent hours playing there after school—and eating soba, of course. These noodles are thinner than spaghetti, tan colored and with a nutty, lightly sweet flavor. To prepare them, hard, grainy buckwheat flour is usually mixed with a little wheat flour to make kneading easier (90/10 is a traditional ratio).

There's nothing like the taste of freshly made soba noodles. At the finest soba restaurants in Tokyo, chefs order buckwheat directly from farmers in the best soba-growing region of the Japanese Alps, then hand-grind the kernels into flour. They prepare a limited amount of noodles a day; when they're out, that's it—they close. This soba haute cuisine inspires such devotion that there are stories of corporate "salarymen" quitting their jobs to apprentice under the top chefs.

Soba's other side is expressed in the humble soba shops that dot the country. These places dish out quick, nutritious meals that are lunchtime favorites, delicious meals I grew up eating, such as Tempura Soba (page 55) and Natto Soba (page 46; natto is another signature food of my region, which I explain in the recipe).

Soba is a popular food in homes, too. In fact, it's woven into the fabric of life in Japan. There's a tradition of serving soba on New Year's Eve—the long noodles symbolize a long life. And it's also a custom to cook soba for new neighbors when you move, as a symbol of a long and happy relationship.

The first recipe that follows is for fresh soba noodles. I encourage you to try them at least once to experience their unique qualities. I'm also including classic family and soba shop recipes, and the ultimate haute cuisine soba recipe, which paradoxically is the simplest one in the section (you'll understand why when you read it). Finally, because soba is so much a part of my soul, I've added my own creations inspired by this versatile noodle.

Soba Noodles

Makes 1½ pounds (serves 4)

My brother-in-law and I have a long-standing ritual whenever I visit my family in Japan: he welcomes me home with a plate of his own freshly made soba noodles. I can't think of a more gracious—and delicious—greeting. I love the bright buckwheat flavor and irresistible nutty, sweet aroma of fresh soba, a sensation you simply can't fully experience with dry noodles or fresh-frozen. This recipe is a bit challenging, true, but worth it.

A few notes: First, professional soba makers use a "soba *kiri*" to cut the noodles, an expensive, specialized blade 12 inches long and 6 inches wide. But at home, a large kitchen knife works perfectly. Second, cooks in Japan traditionally use a lightweight wooden box as a guide for cutting soba, but anything lightweight with a straight edge will work fine, even a plastic ice cube tray. And finally, but most important: cut noodles should be cooked and served immediately. You can freeze any unrolled dough, well wrapped, for up to a month, or store fresh dough in the refrigerator for a few days.

2¼ cups buckwheat flour, plus more for dusting

⅓ cup all-purpose flour

1 cup cold water, plus more if needed

Sift both flours through a sifter or fine-mesh strainer into a large bowl. Add ½ cup of the water and mix well by hand. Slowly add more water and continue mixing until the dough begins to form (it will begin to stick together). The 1 cup of water is just a guide—you may not need to use all of it, or you may need to add more depending on the level of humidity. You want the dough to be smooth and firm, not wet and soft like pizza dough.

Knead the dough by folding the bottom part over the top and pressing down with your entire body weight. Rotate a quarter turn and continue kneading, working the dough until it becomes smooth and shiny, 5 to 6 minutes total.

How do you know when you've kneaded enough? Test the dough by gently stretching a golf ball–size piece between your hands until the dough extends 2 inches before breaking. When you're finished kneading, form the dough into a disk and wrap in plastic. Let it rest at room temperature for 20 minutes.

Once rested, divide the dough into four pieces. Wrap three of the pieces in plastic until you're ready to use them so they won't become dry. Lightly dust your counter with buckwheat flour and set one piece of dough on it. Press down on the dough with your hands until you form a square, then with a rolling pin, roll it into a thin rectangle at least 18 inches long and 1/16 inch thick. Be sure to rotate and flip the dough every few rolls, dusting it with a little flour each time.

Lightly fold to layer the dough into thirds. Gently place a wooden box or straight edge on the dough to use as a guide when cutting the noodles. With a flat knife, cut the layered dough into ⅛-inch-thick strips. Gently shake out the noodles and place them loosely on a plate until ready to use. Repeat with the remaining pieces of dough.

To cook the noodles, place a large pot of water over high heat and bring to a boil. Submerge a metal strainer in the water and add the noodles. Cook for 1 minute or until al dente (tender and cooked through but not mushy). Drain and rinse under cold running water. Serve with Hot or Cold Soba Broth.

Dashi

Makes 2 quarts

Here is my standard dashi recipe. The kelp is loaded with savoriness, a taste we call "umami" in Japan. This recipe is for 2 quarts of dashi, but you can easily double the quantities and freeze leftovers for up to 2 months.

2 large pieces kombu, approximately 10 by 4 inches each, gently wiped with a damp towel

2 quarts plus 1 cup water

3 cups packed katsuobushi (dried bonito flakes)

Place kombu and water in a large stockpot and let it soak at room temperature for at least 20 minutes. You can soak longer, too, even overnight, which will allow the kombu to release more flavor. Bring to a boil over high heat. Remove the kombu and decrease the heat so the liquid is simmering. Add the katsuobushi and gently mix into the liquid; don't stir vigorously. Simmer for 10 minutes longer, then strain through a fine-mesh sieve.

Hot Soba

Serves 4

You can whip up these fast and easy noodles in 15 minutes. They're a typical lunchtime dish in Japan, and the hot soba and broth are especially comforting on a frigid winter day. If you have any leftover chicken, pork, shrimp, or grilled fish in the refrigerator, you can easily add them to this dish, if you'd like. Be sure to shred the chicken or pork. You can also try this soba with cubed firm tofu, which complements the garnishes nicely.

HOT SOBA BROTH

5 cups Dashi (page 40)

½ cup Japanese soy sauce

½ cup mirin

½ cup stemmed and halved enoki mushrooms

ASSEMBLY

12 pea pods, trimmed

14 ounces dried soba noodles

2 scallions, both white and green parts, thinly sliced on an angle

2 sprigs of mitsuba leaves, chopped

Pinch of ichimi togarashi (Japanese red pepper flakes; optional)

Pinch of salt

To make the broth, combine the dashi, soy sauce, and mirin in a stockpot over high heat and bring to a boil. Decrease the heat and simmer for 2 minutes. Add the enoki, cover, and turn off the heat. Keep warm until ready to serve.

To assemble the dish, prepare an ice bath and place a large pot of salted water over high heat. When the water comes to a boil, add the pea pods and cook for 1 minute. Remove the pea pods and submerge in the ice water. Drain.

Place a large pot of water over high heat and bring to a boil. Add the soba noodles, stirring with a fork or chopsticks to make sure the noodles don't stick together. Cook for 4 to 5 minutes, until the noodles are cooked through but al dente. Drain.

To serve, divide the noodles among 4 bowls. Top each with 1¼ cups broth, one-fourth of the enoki mushrooms, scallions, pea pods, and *mitsuba* leaves, and a pinch each of *ichimi togarashi* and salt.

Kaki-Age Soba

Serves 4

Kaki-age is a kind of tempura where a variety of ingredients are mixed with batter and deep-fried. The result is a delicious tempura patty that is paired here with soba and hot broth for a wonderful play of flavors and textures. You'll experience a progression of tastes as you enjoy this dish: a crispy and crunchy patty at first, then the broth infusing it more and more, all the while, the tasty tempura crumbs enhancing the broth.

KAKI-AGE

1 quart vegetable oil

3 large shrimp, peeled and deveined, with tails off, cut into ½-inch pieces

2 large scallops, cut into ½-inch pieces, or 8 bay scallops

½ teaspoon Japanese soy sauce

¼ teaspoon sake

½ carrot, peeled and thinly sliced into 2-inch lengths

3 shiitake mushrooms, stemmed and thinly sliced

¼ onion, thinly sliced

¼ cup chopped mitsuba leaves (you can substitute watercress)

TEMPURA BATTER

1 egg

½ cup water

½ cup plus 2 tablespoons cake flour

14 ounces soba noodles (fresh or dried)

5 cups Hot Soba Broth (page 41)

To prepare the *kaki-age*, heat the vegetable oil in a heavy-bottomed pan or deep fryer to 350°F and bring a pot of water to a boil over high heat.

Combine the shrimp, scallops, soy sauce, and sake in a small bowl and mix well. Set aside.

To make the tempura batter, in a large bowl, lightly beat the egg and water until just combined. Slowly mix in the cake flour, being careful not to overmix—the batter should be thick and slightly frothy, and contain some small lumpy bits of flour. Add more cake flour if the batter is too watery. Fold in the carrot, mushrooms, onion, *mitsuba*, shrimp, and scallops and lightly coat with the batter.

With a large metal spoon, gently slide one-fourth of the mixture into the hot oil, taking care to keep it formed in a small patty. Add a second spoonful and cook both patties for 1½ minutes before flipping and cooking for an additional 1½ to 2 minutes, or until the batter is lightly caramelized and the seafood is cooked through. When you notice the bubbles that appear on the surface of the oil getting smaller and decreasing, and see the patties float to the top, you'll know they're done. Remove the patties from the oil and set on a paper towel–lined tray. Repeat with the remaining mixture to create 2 more *kaki-age* patties.

Cook the soba noodles in the boiling water until al dente, about 1 minute for fresh noodles, or 4 to 5 minutes for dried noodles. Drain well.

To serve, divide the soba noodles among 4 bowls. Top each with 1¼ cups of the hot broth and 1 *kaki-age* patty.

Natto Soba

Serves 4

My hometown of Mito is known throughout Japan as "Natto City" in recognition of our devotion to these fermented soybeans. Natto has a wonderful nutty flavor and aroma, and I've loved it since I was a kid. Serving it with soba is a terrific introduction to this nutritious and ancient naturally preserved ingredient. When you open a packet of natto, the beans will be sticky and thready, but don't let that put you off. This dish makes a beautiful presentation when it's served. Just make sure you mix together all the ingredients very well before you eat to combine the flavors.

14 ounces soba noodles (fresh or dried)

2 (2-ounce) packets natto (fermented soybeans), each one thawed and mixed with 1 teaspoon Japanese soy sauce

⅓ cup shredded nori

½ cup thinly sliced scallions, both white and green parts

1 cup packed katsuobushi (dried bonito flakes)

4 quail eggs

1¼ cups Cold Soba Broth (page 43)

Prepare an ice bath and bring a large pot of water to a boil over high heat. Cook the noodles by placing them in a metal strainer and submerging them in the boiling water. Cook for 1 minute if you're using fresh noodles, or 4 to 5 minutes for dried. Rinse the noodles under cold running water until the water runs clear, then submerge them in the ice bath until cold. Drain well.

Divide the noodles among 4 bowls, and then arrange small mounds of natto, nori, scallions, and katsuobushi over the noodles, lining up the garnishes in a circle. Carefully cut the top off each quail egg using a knife and pour the egg into the center of the garnishes. Serve the cold broth in small cups on the side.

To eat, pour the broth over the noodles and mix all the ingredients with chopsticks until the egg is well incorporated.

Soba Gnocchi with Scallops and Celery Root Foam

Serves 4

This soba gnocchi is one of the most popular dishes at my Chicago restaurant, Takashi. My customers love it and often ask me how to prepare it at home. Well, here's the answer! The recipe is a little challenging, but I guarantee you it will more than impress the guests at your next dinner party. You can prepare the gnocchi in advance, and even freeze it (be sure to coat the gnocchi with vegetable oil before refrigerating or freezing). You can also prepare the celery root sauce ahead of time. And like the gnocchi, you can freeze it, too.

GNOCCHI

1 large Idaho potato

2 tablespoons grated Parmesan cheese

½ teaspoon extra-virgin olive oil

½ lightly beaten egg

½ teaspoon kosher salt

Pinch of white pepper

¼ cup all-purpose flour, plus more for dusting

½ cup buckwheat flour

2 tablespoons vegetable oil

CELERY ROOT FOAM

1 tablespoon extra-virgin olive oil

½ white portion of 1 leek, rinsed well and thinly sliced

¼ onion, thinly sliced

2 cloves garlic, minced

1¾ teaspoons kosher salt

1½ cups cubed celery root

4 cups water

¾ cup half-and-half

1 cup skim milk

1 tablespoon unsalted butter

Pinch of white pepper

ASSEMBLY

¼ cup extra-virgin olive oil

2 royal trumpet mushrooms, cut into quarters lengthwise, then into 2-inch-long pieces

½ teaspoon kosher salt

1 tablespoon unsalted butter

1 tablespoon minced garlic

1 tablespoon minced shallot

½ cup heavy cream

2 tablespoons grated Parmesan cheese

1 tablespoon minced parsley

16 large scallops

Pinch of salt and white pepper

To prepare the gnocchi, preheat the oven to 400°F. Using a fork or the tip of a paring knife, poke several small holes in the potato and place it on a baking sheet. Bake the potato for 1½ hours, or until the potato is very soft to the touch (it should give easily when pressed).

Meanwhile, **begin the celery root foam.** Place a saucepan over medium heat. After 30 seconds, add the olive oil and let it heat for 1 minute, or until it's hot but not smoking. Add the leek, onion, garlic, and ¼ teaspoon of the salt. Decrease the heat to low and cook, stirring often, until the vegetables are translucent, about 5 minutes. Add the celery root and cook for 2 minutes longer. Add the

(continued)

water and bring just to a boil before decreasing the heat to medium-low. Simmer until the celery root becomes soft, about 30 minutes. Remove the saucepan from the heat and let it sit at room temperature until mostly cool, about 15 minutes.

To finish the foam, combine the half-and-half, skim milk, butter, remaining 1½ teaspoons salt, and white pepper in a blender. Add the cooled celery root mixture and blend on high speed until smooth. Strain the sauce through a fine-mesh sieve into a pot. Heat over low heat until the liquid begins to simmer, then turn off the heat and cover to keep warm until ready to use, or if making in advance, cool and reheat later.

To prepare the gnocchi, split the potato in half while still hot. Use a spoon to scoop out the inside, discarding the skin. Grind the potato through a food mill or ricer (you can also use a fine-mesh strainer, but don't use a food processor) and combine it with the Parmesan cheese, olive oil, egg, salt, and pepper. Add the all-purpose and buckwheat flours until you have a smooth, creamy texture, being careful not to overwork the dough.

Dust a work surface with all-purpose flour and divide the dough into 4 portions. Gently roll one portion of the dough on the counter to create a long rope ½ inch thick. Cover the remaining dough with a dry towel.

Lightly pinch the rolled dough between your thumb and index finger. Use a paring knife to cut the dough into 1-inch-long pieces. Each piece should resemble a small pillow (the literal translation of the Italian word *gnocchi*). Repeat with the remaining dough until all has been used.

Prepare an ice bath and bring a large pot of heavily salted water (1 gallon water to ¼ cup salt) to a boil over high heat. Add one-fourth of the gnocchi and cook until the gnocchi have risen to the surface, 1 to 2 minutes (they should be cooked through but still hold their shape). Remove the gnocchi from the water and submerge in the

ice bath. Drain once to cool. Repeat with the remaining gnocchi. Once all the gnocchi have been cooked, lightly toss them with the vegetable oil and refrigerate until ready to use.

To assemble the dish, place a large sauté pan over high heat. Add 2 tablespoons of the olive oil. After 30 seconds, add the mushrooms and salt. Cook until each side of the mushrooms are lightly browned, about 4 minutes, then add the butter. Once melted, add the gnocchi, garlic, and shallot. Cook until the gnocchi are lightly brown. Add the cream and Parmesan cheese. Decrease the heat to low and cook until the sauce has thickened. Stir in the parsley and set aside.

Heat another large sauté pan with the remaining 2 tablespoons olive oil. Season the scallops with a pinch each of salt and pepper, then add to the hot pan. Cook for 1½ to 2 minutes, until the bottoms of the scallops have browned, then turn over and decrease the heat to low. Cook 2 to 2½ minutes longer, or until scallops are cooked to medium.

In a saucepan, heat the foam mixture to a simmer, then transfer it to a tall, narrow container or pot. Use an immersion blender to "foam" the sauce, which will create a layer of bubbles on the surface.

To serve, divide the gnocchi and sauce among 4 shallow bowls. Top each with 4 scallops and ¼ cup foam.

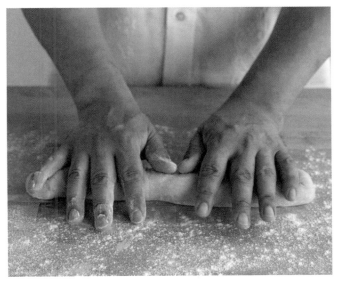

Soba Sushi Two Ways

Serves 4

I still remember the first time I tasted this dish as a child, when my parents took me to a famous shrine near my hometown. Soba sushi was the signature dish there, and restaurants near the shrine served it for lunch. This recipe makes two kinds of soba sushi: soba rolls and *abura-age* sushi. It has a lot of steps, but don't worry, it's not very complicated. The result is worth it: delicious finger food with layers of flavor and texture. Kampyo, the dried squash in the soba rolls, is a traditional ingredient with a delicate sweetness that you can find in Asian markets. Marinated *abura-age* is deep-fried tofu that opens up like pocket bread. Soba sushi is a perfect appetizer or party treat that will wow your guests. This dish also travels well, so you can add it to a lunchbox or picnic basket. You can also prepare this recipe up to a day ahead of serving. Just be sure to wrap it well and store in the refrigerator before serving.

BRAISING LIQUID

1 cup Cold Soba Broth (page 43)

¼ cup sugar

VEGETABLE FILLING

½ cup kampyo (dried squash)

2 cups thinly sliced shiitake mushrooms

½ cup thinly sliced carrots

½ cup diced firm tofu

8 snow peas, trimmed

TAMAGO YAKI

3 eggs

1 tablespoon vegetable oil

BRAISED SOBA NOODLES

1 cup Cold Soba Broth (page 43)

1 teaspoon sesame oil

1 cup cooked soba noodles, drained and cooled

SOBA ROLLS

2 nori sheets

½ cup kampyo (dried squash)

1 tablespoon minced pickled ginger

ABURA-AGE SUSHI

1 tablespoon minced pickled ginger

8 pieces marinated abura-age

To prepare the braising liquid, combine the broth and sugar in a saucepan over high heat. Bring to a boil and stir until the sugar dissolves. Set the braising liquid aside, reserving ¼ cup for the *tamago yaki*.

To prepare the filling, place a large pot of water over high heat and bring to a boil. Add the kampyo and cook until soft, about 20 minutes. Drain.

Combine the kampyo, shiitake mushrooms, carrots, and tofu with the remaining braising liquid and simmer over low heat until all the liquid has been absorbed, 30 to 35 minutes.

Prepare an ice bath and place a pot of salted water over high heat. When the water comes to a boil, add the snow peas. Cook for 30 seconds, then remove and cool in the ice bath. Drain well and thinly slice.

Separate the cooked kampyo from the other braised vegetables and set aside. Divide the rest of the vegetables in

(continued)

half. One part will be used to fill the *abura-age*, the other will be for the nori rolls.

To prepare the *tamago yaki*, whisk together the eggs and the reserved 1/4 cup braising liquid in a bowl. Using a paper towel, lightly coat a 9-inch nonstick sauté pan with the oil and set the pan over high heat. Cook the egg in three batches. Once the oil is hot, add one-third of the egg batter to the pan, then decrease the heat to low and cook for 30 seconds. Gently tilt the pan to spread the egg into a thin layer like a crêpe, cooking for 1 minute. Carefully lift the edges to make sure the egg doesn't stick, and cook until the bottom has caramelized, about 1 minute longer. Use a flat-bottomed spatula to flip over the *tamago yaki*; cook until the bottom is dry, about 15 seconds longer. Remove the *tamago yaki* from the pan and set it on a paper towel to cool. Repeat with the remaining egg batter in two more batches.

Once all 3 *tamago yaki* have cooled, cut each into thirds, then thinly slice. Divide the sliced *tamago yaki* in half and set aside.

To prepare the soba noodles, prepare an ice bath. Bring the broth and sesame oil to a boil in a small saucepan. Add the cooked noodles and cook for 10 seconds. Cool the noodles and broth together in the ice bath (place the entire saucepan in the ice bath). Once cool, divide in half.

To make the soba rolls, begin by gathering the pickled ginger, the reserved cooked kampyo, half of the vegetable filling, half of the *tamago yaki* and half of the soba noodles. Then, divide each of these in half for making two rolls. Place 1 sheet of nori horizontally over a piece of plastic wrap (which should be longer and wider than the nori). Place half of the vegetable filling in an even, lengthwise row about 1 inch above the bottom of the nori. Now lay half of the kampyo along the length of the nori and cut to fit. Contiue to layer with half of the *tamago yaki*, soba noodles, and pickled ginger. Using the palstic wrap as a guide, roll the nori from the bottom, being sure to create a tight roll. Keep the plastic on the roll so it stays secure.

Repeat with the remaining portions of the vegetable filling, kampyo, *tamago yaki*, soba noodles, and pickled ginger to make another roll.

Cut each roll in half, then cut each piece in half again to make 16 pieces total. Remove from the plastic before serving.

To make the *abura-age* sushi, combine the remaining vegetable filling, *tamago yaki*, and soba noodles in a large bowl with the pickled ginger. Stuff each *abura-age* with 2 tablespoons of the mixture, being sure to leave enough room so the opening edges overlap. Set on a tray with the open side down.

Tempura Soba

Serves 4

Tempura soba is a delicious and satisfying lunchtime favorite in Japan, served both at home and in restaurants across the country. Tempura has a long history in the country. The cooking method was introduced by the Portuguese in the sixteenth century and has been refined into a uniquely Japanese food ever since. Make sure you eat this dish quickly, while the soba is still steaming and the tempura is hot and crispy. The way we enjoy this dish in Japan is to dip the tempura into the soba broth as we eat it. This serves two purposes: First, the broth flavors the tempura, acting as a dipping sauce. And second, the tempura returns the favor, adding richness to the broth while its crumbs add texture. So we have both foods working together to create an irresistible whole!

1 quart vegetable oil, or enough to fill a pot or deep fryer 3 inches deep

5 cups Hot Soba Broth (page 41)

1 egg

1¼ cups cold water

2 cups cake flour, plus more for dusting

8 large shrimp, peeled and deveined, with tails on

8 small shiitake mushrooms, stemmed

4 asparagus stalks, ends trimmed, cut into thirds

14 ounces dried soba noodles

2 scallions, both white and green parts, thinly sliced on an angle

Heat the vegetable oil in a deep fryer or heavy-bottomed saucepan to 350°F. Also fill a medium pot with water and bring to a boil over high heat.

Heat the broth in a saucepan over medium heat until it comes to a boil. Lower the heat, cover, and keep warm until ready to serve.

Prepare the tempura batter by beating the egg and water in a bowl. Mix well and then slowly mix in the 2 cups flour until just combined. Be careful not to overmix; you don't want a smooth batter like pancake batter. Instead, you want tiny lumps of flour to remain in the batter.

With a sharp knife, make five shallow slits across the underside of each shrimp. Next, flip the shrimp over so their undersides are resting against your cutting board. Now gently press down on the shrimp with your fingers to flatten slightly. This action will stop the shrimp from curling when you cook them, but be careful not to press too hard because the shrimp could break into pieces.

Dip the shrimp, mushrooms, and asparagus into the tempura batter, and carefully place in the hot oil. Cook the vegetables for about 3 minutes and the shrimp for 1 minute longer. When you notice the bubbles that appear on the surface of the oil getting smaller and decreasing, and see the ingredients float to the top, you'll know they're done. The color of the tempura will be a light golden brown—make sure the tempura doesn't overcook and turn dark brown. Transfer the ingredients from the oil and rest on a paper towel–lined tray to absorb any extra oil.

Add the soba noodles to the pot of boiling water, stirring with a fork or chopsticks to make sure the noodles don't stick together. Boil for 4 to 5 minutes, or until the noodles are just cooked through but still al dente. Drain well.

To serve, divide the soba noodles among 4 soup bowls, add the broth, and garnish with the scallions. Serve the tempura on a separate plate.

Tempura Shrimp-Stuffed Zucchini Blossoms with Soba

Serves 4

Zucchini blossoms are an ingredient that always catches my eye in the early summertime, especially at the farmers' markets here in my hometown of Chicago. They inspired me to come up with this recipe, my own interpretation of the classic stuffed zucchini blossoms of both Italian and Japanese cuisines. In this dish, I stuff the flowers with onion and shrimp, then fry them as tempura, a combination of flavors and textures that complements the toothsome soba.

1 quart plus ¼ cup vegetable oil

¼ cup minced onion

10 large shrimp, peeled and deveined, with tails off

2 egg yolks

½ teaspoon salt

½ teaspoon pepper

12 zucchini blossoms

4 cups Hot Soba Broth (page 41)

8 asparagus stalks, ends trimmed and cut into thirds

12 ounces dried soba noodles

2 scallions, both white and green parts, thinly sliced

TEMPURA BATTER

2 eggs

1 cup water

1¼ cups cake flour, plus ½ cup for dusting

Heat the 1 quart vegetable oil in a deep fryer or heavy-bottomed sauepan to 325°F.

In a small bowl, cover the minced onion in cold water and soak for 10 minutes. To drain, wrap the onion in a paper towel and squeeze to remove excess moisture.

With a heavy knife, finely chop the shrimp until it begins to form a paste. There should still be small lumps of shrimp—it shouldn't be completely smooth.

In a bowl, combine the onion and shrimp and mix well with a rubber spatula. In another bowl, whisk together the egg yolks and the remaining ¼ cup vegetable oil (like making mayonnaise), and then combine well with the shrimp, and add the salt and pepper. Transfer the filling to a pastry bag.

Trim the stems of the zucchini blossoms and remove the pistils (the yellow pollen inside). Cut a small hole in the bottom of the pastry bag and pipe the shrimp mixture into a zucchini blossom until very full (about 1 tablespoon per blossom). Overlap the edges of the blossom to seal in the filling and set aside. Repeat with the remaining blossoms.

(continued)

Prepare the tempura batter by beating together the eggs and water. Add 1¼ cups of the cake flour and mix together. The batter should be well combined but still have a few lumps.

Bring a large pot of water to a boil over high heat. Also heat the broth over high heat. When the broth comes to a boil, reduce the heat to low and cover to keep warm.

Pour the remaining ½ cup cake flour onto a small bowl. Lightly dust the asparagus in the flour, then dip the pieces into the tempura batter. Carefully drop the asparagus into the fryer and cook for 1½ to 2 minutes, or until cooked through, making sure the batter doesn't turn brown. Remove from the fryer and place the asparagus on a paper towel–lined plate to drain excess oil.

Dust the stuffed zucchini blossoms with the flour and dip into the tempura batter. Fry the zucchini blossoms for 3 minutes, or until the filling is cooked through. Place on a paper towel–lined plate to drain the excess oil.

Cook the soba noodles in the boiling water for 4 or 5 minutes, or until the noodles are just cooked through but still al dente. Drain well.

To serve, divide the soba noodles among 4 bowls. Top each with 1 cup hot broth and one-fourth of the asparagus and zucchini blossoms. Garnish with the sliced scallions.

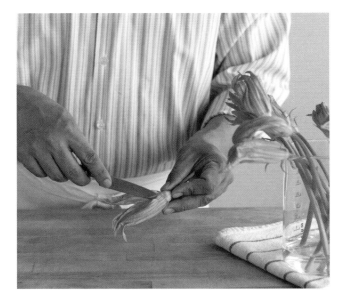

Prepare the tempura batter by beating together the eggs and water. Add 1¼ cups of the cake flour and mix together. The batter should be well combined but still have a few lumps.

Bring a large pot of water to a boil over high heat. Also heat the broth over high heat. When the broth comes to a boil, reduce the heat to low and cover to keep warm.

Pour the remaining ½ cup cake flour onto a small bowl. Lightly dust the asparagus in the flour, then dip the pieces into the tempura batter. Carefully drop the asparagus into the fryer and cook for 1½ to 2 minutes, or until cooked through, making sure the batter doesn't turn brown. Remove from the fryer and place the asparagus on a paper towel–lined plate to drain excess oil.

Dust the stuffed zucchini blossoms with the flour and dip into the tempura batter. Fry the zucchini blossoms for 3 minutes, or until the filling is cooked through. Place on a paper towel–lined plate to drain the excess oil.

Cook the soba noodles in the boiling water for 4 or 5 minutes, or until the noodles are just cooked through but still al dente. Drain well.

To serve, divide the soba noodles among 4 bowls. Top each with 1 cup hot broth and one-fourth of the asparagus and zucchini blossoms. Garnish with the sliced scallions.

Tororo Soba

Serves 4

This summer recipe centers on a versatile ingredient that's beloved in Japan but almost unknown here, one that I know you'll enjoy. It's called *yamaimo*, or mountain yam. This root has a nice, fresh taste, with a delicately sweet, nutty flavor and lots of umami, or sense of savoriness. The most popular variety, which you can find in Asian markets, looks like a tan-colored baton. Peel the skin and grate its white flesh. Raw *yamaimo* has a liquidy, slippery texture that might take getting used to, but it pairs beautifully with the toothsome soba in this dish. I've also added okra, a cooling Southern favorite that's very popular in Japan.

GARNISHES

8 pieces okra

1 sheet nori, broken into small pieces

½ cup daikon sprouts (also referred to as radish sprouts)

8 obha leaves, stemmed and thinly sliced

14 ounces soba noodles (fresh or dried)

4 teaspoons wasabi paste

1¼ cups Cold Soba Broth (page 43)

½ cup grated yamaimo (Japanese mountain yam)

To prepare the garnishes, ready an ice bath and place a pot of salted water over high heat. When the water comes to a boil, add the okra and cook for 1½ minutes, or until it turns bright green. Submerge in the ice bath to cool. Drain, pat dry, and slice into ¼-inch-thick pieces.

Bring a large pot of water to a boil over high heat. Place the soba noodles in a metal strainer and submerge in the boiling water. Cook for 1 minute if you're using fresh noodles, or 4 to 5 minutes for dried. Rinse the noodles under cold running water until the water runs clear, then immerse in the ice bath until cool. Drain well.

Divide the noodles among 4 plates and dab 1 teaspoon of wasabi on the side of each plate. Garnish with okra, nori, daikon sprouts, and *obha* leaves. Divide the broth among 4 cups and mix each with 2 tablespoons of the *yamaimo*.

To eat, add the wasabi to the broth to taste, then dip the noodles into the broth with your chopsticks.

Wakame Soba

Serves 4

Loaded with nutrients, wakame has been an important part of the Japanese diet for centuries. And besides being good for you, it has a wonderful flavor that's both briny and sweet. I love this seaweed and eat a ton of it. Wakame is also very convenient: because it's dried, it can be stored for months, but it takes only minutes to reconstitute. This quick and easy soba dish is a delicious way to introduce this versatile ingredient to American cooks, especially when paired with fresh snow peas and tangy onions. Give it a try; I know you'll love wakame as much as I do.

3 tablespoons dried wakame

3 cups hot water

16 snow peas, trimmed

¼ red onion

14 ounces soba noodles (fresh or dried)

4 cups Hot Soba Broth (page 41)

In a bowl, cover the wakame with the hot water and let sit for 10 minutes. Drain well and set aside.

Prepare an ice bath and bring a small pot of salted water to a boil. Also bring a pot of water to a boil. Cook the snow peas in the salted water for 1 minute, then submerge in the ice bath. Cool, drain, and cut in half.

Thinly slice the red onion into rounds, about ½ cup. In a small bowl, cover the onion with cold water for 5 minutes. Drain well.

Cook the soba noodles in the unsalted boiling water until al dente, about 1 minute for fresh noodles, or 4 or 5 minutes for dried. Drain well.

To serve, divide the noodles among 4 bowls and top each with 1 cup hot broth. Garnish each with one-fourth of the snow peas, red onion, and wakame, and stir gently.

CHAPTER THREE | Udon

UDON

HERE in America we don't often think of Japan as a country with cultural divides as strong as the ones north and south of the Mason-Dixon Line. But Japan is indeed a land of distinct regional identities, and Osaka, the largest city in the western part of the country, distinctly stands apart from Tokyo in attitude, personality, dialect—and noodles. Osaka and southern Japan are the traditional home to udon, flavorful white noodles made from wheat flour. Udon inspires similar devotion in the south that soba does up north, although it's considered a more down-to-earth noodle.

Even though I'm from the Tokyo area, I love udon noodles (don't tell anyone). Today, Japanese noodles of every stripe, of course, are enjoyed throughout the country. My wife and kids also are crazy for udon, which have a silkier, smoother texture than soba and are easy to slurp down.

Like ramen and soba, udon inspires feverish devotion in Japan. To get an idea of just how feverish, head to a small city called Takamatsu on the island of Shikoku. According to legend, a Buddhist monk brought udon to this area from China in the ninth century. Today, its citizens are said, on average, to slurp down a remarkable 230 bowls of *sanuki* udon a year, as the local thick and chewy noodles are called, the highest per capita consumption of udon in the country. And it's not just for the locals. This city's a major tourist destination, boasting hundreds of *sanuki* udon restaurants and "udon taxis" to ferry visitors on a noodle crawl to the most famous ones. Tourists here can still witness the traditional method of kneading udon dough—the chef stomping on it with his or her stockinged feet.

Although udon is a simple food, interestingly enough, hundreds of years ago it was considered a dish for nobility, more high class than soba. I can understand why. To me, these slippery noodles are the perfect complement to fresh ingredients and flavors. In the recipes that follow, you'll see I have fun pairing different tastes and textures to create elegant dishes influenced by my contemporary French and American cooking. I also include classic udon recipes that are standard in every corner of Japan.

Udon Broth

Makes 3½ cups

While the underlying dashi is the same, udon broth is not as strongly flavored as soba broth because these wheat flour noodles absorb liquid easier than do the hard buckwheat of soba. You can freeze this broth for up to a month or keep in the refrigerator for up to a week and use for a number of dishes, which is what we do at my home because my family is crazy for udon!

3 cups Dashi (page 40)
½ cup plus 2 tablespoons Japanese soy sauce
½ cup mirin

Combine all the ingredients in a saucepan and bring to a boil. Decrease the heat and keep warm until ready to serve.

Su Udon

Su means "plain" in Japanese, which is how this dish got its name. But plain doesn't mean boring—this is a simple and light dish that I love when I want to enjoy the chewy texture of udon noodles without eating anything too heavy. Wakame is a nutritious seaweed that's found in many Japanese dishes. You can include spinach in this recipe, too, if you'd like. Just quickly blanch the spinach in boiling water, cool in an ice bath, and drain before adding to the individual bowls.

6 cups Udon Broth (page 66)

4 shiitake mushrooms, stems removed and halved

2 tablespoons dried wakame

1 cup hot water

1 pound dried udon noodles

¼ cup mitsuba, cut into 1-inch-long pieces, including stems

2 scallions, both white and green parts, thinly sliced on an angle

Bring a large pot of water to a boil over high heat.

Place the broth in a pot over medium heat and bring to a simmer. Add the mushrooms and simmer for 1 minute, then decrease the heat to low and cover to keep warm.

In a bowl, cover the wakame with the hot water and let sit for 10 minutes. Drain well and set aside.

Cook the udon noodles in the boiling water until al dente, following the package instructions. Drain well. Divide the noodles among 4 bowls and pour 1½ cups of the broth over each. Garnish the bowls with one-quarter of the mushrooms, wakame, *mitsuba*, and scallions.

Curry Udon

Serves 4

Japanese *curry*? Actually, curry has been a part of Japanese cuisine for more than a hundred years. The Japanese navy adopted it in the nineteenth century from their British counterparts, who ate it on ships. Soon, eating curry on Friday became a Japanese naval tradition. And not just for sailors. Japanese citizens fell in love with curry, too, especially kids. I should know—I was one of them. When I was growing up, I was crazy about curry. Now my own kids adore it, especially in this dish. You can use any cut of beef that you like. If you want to go upscale, try rib eye, but even beef scraps work just fine.

1½ tablespoons vegetable oil

1 cup thinly sliced yellow onion

1 cup peeled and thinly sliced salsify

1 teaspoon curry powder

6 cups Udon Broth (page 66)

3 ounces medium-hot Japanese curry sauce mix

1¼ cups whole milk

12 ounces beef, sliced paper thin (ask your butcher to slice it for you)

1 pound dried udon noodles

2 scallions, both white and green parts, thinly sliced

8 mitsuba leaves, thinly sliced

Set a large sauté or wide-bottomed pan over high heat and add 1½ tablespoons of the oil. When the oil is hot, about 30 seconds, add the onions and salsify. Cook for 1 minute, then decrease the heat to medium and cook, stirring often, until the onions are soft, approximately 45 seconds longer. Add the curry powder and continue cooking, stirring often, until it has been absorbed, about 30 seconds.

Pour the broth over the vegetables and increase the heat to high. Add the curry sauce mix and stir until dissolved, about 2 minutes. Stir in the milk and heat for 1 minute. Stir in the beef and cook over medium heat until the meat is cooked through, 2½ to 3 minutes.

Place a large pot of water over high heat and bring to a boil. Add the noodles and cook, following package instructions. Drain well. Divide the noodles among 4 bowls. Into each bowl pour one-fourth of the curry broth and the beef and garnish with the scallions and *mitsuba* leaves.

Chilled Inaniwa Udon with Heirloom Tomatoes and Ratatouille

Serves 4

Save this dish for late summer, when tomatoes and vegetables are at their peak of flavor. Use a variety of heirloom tomatoes, especially ones with different colors, which will make for an eye-catching presentation. *Inaniwa* udon is a noodle that originated in Japan's rugged far north. Unlike typical udon noodles, which look like thick spaghetti, *inaniwa* is shaped like linguine and tastes great chilled.

½ cup chopped red onion (½-inch pieces)

1 cup cubed zucchini (½-inch cubes)

½ cup chopped red bell pepper (½-inch pieces)

2 cups peeled and cubed eggplant (½-inch cubes)

½ cup plus 2 tablespoons extra-virgin olive oil

2 cloves garlic, thinly sliced

1 pound dried inaniwa udon noodles

½ cup balsamic vinegar

2 tablespoons Japanese soy sauce

Pepper

⅔ cup thinly sliced basil

2 cups cubed assorted heirloom tomatoes (1-inch cubes)

1 cup arugula

½ cup grated Parmesan cheese

½ cup roughly chopped toasted pine nuts

Combine the red onion, zucchini, bell pepper, and eggplant in a large bowl and cover with cold water. Soak the vegetables for 10 minutes, then drain.

Heat ½ cup of the olive oil in a large sauté pan over medium heat for 1 minute, then add the vegetables and garlic. Sauté, stirring often, until the vegetables are cooked through but not too soft, about 8 minutes. Transfer the vegetables to a bowl and refrigerate until cool, about 20 minutes.

Place a large pot of water over high heat and bring to a boil. Add the noodles and cook until al dente, following package instructions. Then transfer the noodles to a colander or fine-mesh sieve and rinse well under cold water. Drain and set aside.

Finish the vegetables by stirring in the balsamic vinegar, soy sauce, and the remaining 2 tablespoons olive oil. Season with a few grinds of pepper, then mix in the basil.

To assemble the dish, divide the noodles among 4 plates and top each with one-fourth of the heirloom tomatoes followed by the vegetable mixture, arugula, Parmesan, and pine nuts.

Spicy Eggplant Ja-Ja-Men Udon

Serves 4

Everyone in Japan knows *ja-ja-men*, with its spicy miso and garlicky flavors. Think of it as the Japanese version of spaghetti and Bolognese sauce, a favorite at home and casual restaurants. This may sound counterintuitive, but I love eating this dish on a hot summer day—its spices reenergize me.

2 cups peeled cubed eggplant (½-inch cubes)

½ cup chopped green bell pepper (½-inch pieces)

⅓ cup drained canned bamboo shoots, cut into ½-inch pieces

4 scallions, green and white parts separated

3 tablespoons sake

2 tablespoons aka miso (red miso)

2 tablespoons tahini (sesame paste)

6 tablespoons Japanese soy sauce

2 tablespoons tobanjan (Chinese chili paste)

5 tablespoons mirin

½ cup Dashi (page 40)

1 teaspoon cornstarch

1 teaspoon water

2 tablespoons vegetable oil

1 tablespoon minced garlic

1 tablespoon minced ginger

8 ounces ground pork

2 tablespoons sesame oil

1 pound dried udon noodles

Combine the eggplant, bell pepper, and bamboo shoots in a bowl and cover with cold water. Soak for 10 minutes, then drain well. In the meantime, mince the green parts of the scallions and thinly slice the white parts on an angle, and set aside.

Combine the sake, miso, tahini, soy sauce, *tobanjan*, mirin, and dashi in a bowl and set aside. In a small bowl or cup, mix together the cornstarch and water to make a smooth paste, and set aside.

Heat the vegetable oil in a sauté pan set over medium-high heat. Add the garlic and ginger. Cook, stirring constantly, until the garlic is golden brown, about 2 minutes.

Add the pork and minced green scallion. Use a wooden spatula to combine these ingredients with the garlic and ginger. Cook for 3 minutes, then add the vegetables and cook for 1 minute longer. Add the sesame oil and decrease the heat to medium. Cook for 3 minutes longer, constantly stirring to combine the pork.

Add the sake and miso mixture, mixing well. Add the cornstarch mixture (be sure to whisk it again if the cornstarch and water have separated). Stir well and cook until the sauce thickens, about 2 minutes. Remove from the heat.

Place a large pot of water over high heat and bring to a boil. Add the udon noodles and cook, following package instructions. Drain well. Divide the noodles among 4 plates.

Return the sauce to the stove top and set over medium heat; stir until the sauce is heated through, then pour one-fourth of the sauce over each plate. Garnish each with 1 tablespoon of the reserved sliced white scallion.

Kitsune Udon

Serves 4

My kids can't get enough of the savory and sweet flavor of this dish, which makes me smile because I still remember the moment I first tasted *kitsune* udon—in elementary school. Back in Japan, my grade school served meals to its students, and these noodles were one of my favorite lunchtime treats. I know both you and your kids will love them, too: they're easy to prepare and the sweet and tangy flavor lasts and lasts.

ABURA-AGE

2 packs (2 large pieces each) marinated abura-age (fried bean curd), halved

6 cups water

2 cups Dashi (page 40)

¼ cup sugar

2 tablespoons mirin

2 tablespoons Japanese soy sauce

6 cups Udon Broth (page 66)

1 pound dried udon noodles

3 scallions, both white and green parts chopped, for garnish

To prepare the *abura-age,* in a medium saucepan, add the *abura-age* and water. Bring to a boil, then drain the *abura-age*; rinse with cold water and gently squeeze out excess water. Place the *abura-age* back in the same pan and add the dashi, sugar, mirin, and soy sauce; set over medium heat. Simmer the liquid to reduce until nearly all of it has evaporated, 8 to 10 minutes.

Heat the broth in a small pot over medium heat. Once it comes to a boil, cover the pot and decrease the heat to low. Keep warm until ready to serve.

Place a large pot of water over high heat and bring to a boil. Add the udon noodles and cook, following package instructions. Drain well.

Divide the noodles among 4 bowls. Pour one-fourth of the hot broth into each bowl. Top each with 1 piece *abura-age* and garnish by sprinkling the scallions over the top.

Egg Drop and Crab Nabeyaki Udon

Serves 4

Winter is the best season to enjoy this dish, when crab is at its most flavorful. I love serving these noodles in individual clay pots, which are such an intimate and satisfying way to enjoy a meal. These vessels become very hot when you cook in them, though, so be careful when you remove them from the burners. If you don't have a clay pot, you can use other vessels, too. (See the discussion on clay pots in the recipce for Somen in a Clay Pot with Chicken and Eggplant, page 90, for more information.) Timing is very important for this dish to cook correctly, so make sure you have your game plan ready before you start.

1 pound dried udon noodles

3 quarts Udon Broth (page 66)

1⅓ cups peeky toe crabmeat (or substitute with any type of crabmeat)

½ cup spring peas

4 eggs, kept separated, lightly beaten

4 obha leaves, thinly sliced

1 tablespoon thinly sliced yuzu peel (or substitute with lemon zest)

1 cup chopped mitsuba leaves (1-inch pieces)

Place a large pot of water over high heat and bring to a boil. Add the udon noodles and cook, following package instructions. Drain well and set aside.

Divide the broth among 4 clay pots and heat over mecium-high heat. Bring the broth to a boil, then decrease the heat and simmer.

To each clay pot, add one-fourth of the cooked noodles and simmer for 30 seconds. Add one-fourth of the crabmeat and peas and pour 1 beaten egg over the top. Immediately turn off the heat (the broth will continue boiling) and garnish with the *obha* leaves, yuzu, and *mitsuba* leaves.

Carefully remove the clay pots from the stove top and set on heat-resistant plates. Serve immediately.

Niku Udon

Serves 4

In Japan, this udon is a rich and comforting wintertime favorite, and it is especially popular with young people. And not only in Japan. Here in Chicago, it's one of my son's favorites. He plays ice hockey in school, and when he comes home after practice he's ravenous. *Niku* udon to the rescue, every time.

5 cups Udon Broth (page 66)

8 ounces beef, thinly sliced

½ cup sliced firm tofu (¼ by ¼ by 1-inch pieces)

2 scallions, both white and green parts, cut into 1-inch pieces

1 pound dried udon noodles

½ cup watercress

Pour the broth into a small saucepan. Place over medium-high heat and bring to a simmer. One at a time, dip each slice of beef into the broth and cook for 5 to 10 seconds. Remove the beef from the broth and place on a dish. Cover the dish to keep warm.

Add the tofu and scallions to the simmering broth and cook for 1 minute. Decrease the heat to low and cover to keep warm.

Place a large pot of water over high heat and bring to a boil. Add the noodles and cook, following package instructions. Drain well and divide the noodles among 4 bowls.

To serve, top each bowl of noodles with one-fourth of the broth, tofu, scallions, and beef. Garnish with the watercress.

Poached Egg and Mentaiko Udon

Serves 4

Here's one for the grown-ups. In Japan, we usually don't drink sake or beer without a salty or spicy dish to tickle the palate. This udon is both salty *and* spicy, and is a perfect complement to your favorite beverage. The poached egg yolk in the dish adds a satisfying richness to the broth.

1 cup Udon Broth (page 66)

1 tablespoon rice vinegar

4 eggs

1 pound dried udon noodles

¼ cup Japanese soy sauce

¼ cup mentaiko (spicy fish roe), membrane peeled

½ cup cooked kombu, chilled (saved from preparing dashi), thinly sliced

4 sprigs mitsuba, cut into 1-inch lengths

In a saucepan, heat the broth just to a boil. Decrease the heat and cover to keep warm until ready to serve.

Bring a pot of water to a simmer (200°F) and add the rice vinegar. Crack 1 egg into a small bowl, then carefully slide it into the water. Wait 1 minute, then repeat with the remaining eggs, adding each in 1-minute intervals. Cook each egg for 3 to 4 minutes, until partially cooked through but the yolk is still soft. Remove the eggs from the water with a slotted spoon to a bowl and cover.

Place a large pot of water over high heat and bring to a boil. Add the noodles and cook until al dente, following package instructions. Drain well.

Divide the noodles among 4 bowls. Top each with ¼ cup warm broth and 1 tablespoon soy sauce. Add 1 poached egg to each bowl and garnish with the *mentaiko*, kombu, and *mitsuba*.

To eat, combine thoroughly with chopsticks.

Yaki Udon

Serves 2

This dish is perfect for anyone with a hearty appetite. In Japan, it's especially popular with teenagers, who devour large plates of these satisfying and filling fried noodles. Yaki udon is also a staple of Japan's *izakaya*, or eating pubs, especially as a late night snack or complement to a frosty mug of beer. This recipe works best in servings of two. If you'd like to make it for four people, just prepare the dish in two batches.

¼ cup dried wood ear mushrooms

3 tablespoons vegetable oil

2 ounces pork belly, thinly sliced

6 large shrimp, peeled and deveined, with tails off, cut into
½-inch pieces

¼ cup sliced lotus root (renkon)

⅓ cup thinly sliced carrots (1-inch by 2-inch rectangles,
⅛ inch thick)

2 cups chopped napa cabbage

½ thinly sliced onion

¼ cup sliced bamboo shoots

¼ cup stemmed enoki mushrooms

¼ cup shimeji mushrooms

½ cup Udon Broth (page 66)

2 tablespoons Japanese soy sauce

1 teaspoon sesame oil

18 ounces frozen udon noodles (2 packages), thawed

Pinch of kosher salt

Pinch of black pepper

¼ cup finely shaved katsuobushi (bonito flakes)

Rehydrate the wood ear mushrooms by soaking in hot water for 10 minutes. Drain the liquid and set aside.

Set a large sauté pan over high heat. Add 2 tablespoons of the vegetable oil and heat until the oil just begins to smoke. Add the pork and shrimp; cook for 1½ to 2 minutes, stirring often, until the shrimp just turn pink but neither is cooked through. Transfer the cooked pork and shrimp to a plate but keep the oil in the pan.

With the pan over high heat, add the lotus root, carrots, cabbage, onions, bamboo shoots, and wood ear, enoki, and shimeji mushrooms. Add the remaining 1 tablespoon oil, if necessary. Cook until the vegetables are tender, 2 to 4 minutes.

Reduce the heat to medium and add the broth, soy sauce, and sesame oil to the vegetables. Cook for 2 minutes longer, or until most of the liquid has evaporated.

Place a large pot of water over high heat and bring to a boil. Add the noodles and cook for 1 minute, just long enough to heat through. Drain well.

Add the noodles to the pan with the vegetables, then add the pork and shrimp. Mix well and cook for 1 to 2 minutes longer, until the shrimp and pork are fully cooked and the vegetables are soft. Season with the salt and black pepper.

To serve, divide the noodles between 2 plates. Garnish with the katsuobushi.

CHAPTER FOUR | # Somen

SOMEN

LIKE udon, somen is a wheat noodle with a long history in Japan. Somen, though, is as thin as angel hair pasta, which makes it quick and convenient to prepare. When I was growing up, that meant one thing: summertime eating. When it was hot and steamy outside, my mother would prepare somen for my family almost every day.

Somen is still my favorite noodle in the summer, especially with the dipping sauces I describe in this section. In Japan, we eat these noodles chilled, and even add a few ice cubes to the plates to keep them cool. They're refreshing and light, and you don't have to spend too much time over a hot stove to prepare a somen dish (the noodles cook in 1 minute).

But just because they're easy to cook doesn't mean they're boring. In addition to the delicious dipping sauces, chilled somen complements seafood especially well, as you'll see in the following recipes. You can also simply add any leftovers you might have, such as shredded chicken, to my basic somen recipe. By varying the garnishes, you can serve somen all summer long and never tire of it—another trick I learned from my mother. Finally, I've included a year-round recipe cooked in individual clay pots, which will wow any guest when presented at the table.

Somen

Serves 4

This recipe is for somen at its most elementary: a simple but sublime combination of noodles accented with a mixture of aromatic garnishes. You can layer other ingredients in this dish if you'd like, too, such as steamed and cooled spinach, fava beans or sugar snap peas, or thinly sliced raw carrots (find the freshest carrots you can, especially from your garden or farmers' market). Just add it to the garnish dish. Cooling the broth in a metal container, as I recommend below, will help the liquid chill faster.

SOMEN BROTH

½ cup **Dashi (page 40)**
¼ cup **mirin**
¼ cup **Japanese soy sauce**

GARNISHES

2 teaspoons **grated ginger**
4 **obha leaves, thinly sliced**
2 **scallions, both white and green parts, thinly sliced on an angle**
4 **sprigs mitsuba, cut into 1-inch lengths**

14 ounces **dried somen noodles**
½ cup **ice cubes**

To make the broth, first prepare an ice bath. Combine all the broth ingredients in a small saucepan. Place over high heat and bring just to a boil. Turn off the heat and transfer the broth to a metal container. Place the container in the ice bath until the broth is chilled.

Divide the garnishes among 4 small dishes.

Place a large pot of water over high heat and bring to a boil. Add the somen noodles and cook, following package instructions. Drain and rinse well under cold running water.

To serve, divide the noodles among 4 plates and top each with a few ice cubes, which will prevent the noodles from sticking together. Pour ¼ cup of the somen broth into each of 4 small cups. Serve the noodles and broth alongside the garnishes.

To eat, mix the garnishes into the broth and dip the noodles in with chopsticks.

Cold Somen Dipping Sauces

Makes 1½ cups of each

Here are the six basic dipping sauces that I use for my cold somen recipes. Because these noodles are typically a summertime dish, the sauces are designed to be whipped up in a snap, without too much work in a hot kitchen! Each dipping sauce recipe makes 4 portions and should be served with 12 ounces of dried somen noodles, cooked and chilled. You can prepare the somen broth ahead of time, and it freezes very well. But be sure to serve the dipping sauces fresh, preparing them just before you cook the noodles. That way you get the best flavors out of the ingredients.

COLD SOMEN BROTH

¾ cup Dashi (page 40)

6 tablespoons mirin

6 tablespoons Japanese soy sauce

Combine all the ingredients in a pot set over high heat and bring just to a boil. Remove from the heat and chill.

YAMAIMO

1¼ cups Cold Somen Broth (above)

½ cup grated yamaimo (Japanese mountain yam)

½ teaspoon wasabi paste

½ piece nori, thinly sliced (or you can buy precut nori confetti)

Divide the broth among 4 small cups. Add one-fourth of the *yamaimo* to each and garnish with a dab of the wasabi paste and some slices of nori.

GOMA

6 tablespoons goma paste (can substitute with tahini, or grind toasted sesame seeds to a paste in a coffee grinder)

1¼ cups Cold Somen Broth (above)

Combine the goma paste and broth in a bowl and whisk until well combined. Divide among 4 cups and serve.

YUZU

4 teaspoons yuzu juice (or substitute with lemon juice)

½ teaspoon yuzu pepper (or substitute with capers)

1 teaspoon minced yuzu peel (or substitute with lemon zest)

1¼ cups Cold Somen Broth (above)

Combine all the ingredients in a bowl and mix well. Divide among 4 cups and serve.

SHISO-UME

4 obha leaves

6 umeboshi (pickled Japanese apricots), pitted

1¼ cups Cold Somen Broth (above)

Lay the *obha* leaves over the umeboshi and mash with a heavy knife until it forms a paste. Whisk the paste into the broth. Divide among 4 cups and serve.

TOMATO

2 Roma tomatoes

2 tablespoons minced cilantro

2 tablespoons extra-virgin olive oil

6 tablespoons rice vinegar

6 tablespoons Cold Somen Broth (above)

½ teaspoon yuzu pepper (can substitute with capers)

Prepare an ice bath and bring a small pot of water to a boil.

With a paring knife, remove the core from the tomatoes and lightly score an X on the bottom. Place the tomatoes in the boiling water for 10 seconds, then remove and submerge in the ice bath for 10 seconds. Once again place the tomatoes in the boiling water (a second time), now for 5 seconds, and then submerge in the ice bath until cool.

Once the tomatoes have chilled, peel the skin, then cut into quarters. Use a tablespoon to scrape out the seeds, which you'll discard, then chop the tomatoes into small pieces.

In a bowl, combine the tomatoes with the cilantro, olive oil, rice vinegar, broth, and yuzu pepper and mix well. Divide among 4 small cups and serve.

WALNUT

1¼ cups walnuts

1¼ cups Cold Somen Broth (page 86)

Preheat the oven to 350°F. Spread the walnuts on a baking sheet and place in the oven until lightly toasted, about 5 minutes. Remove from the baking sheet and cool.

Grind the walnuts into a smooth paste with a food processor or coffee grinder. This should make 6 tablespoons.

Pour the broth into a bowl. Start whisking the liquid and slowly add the walnut paste to combine. Divide among 4 small cups and serve.

Somen

Grilled Salmon and Chilled Somen with Yuzu Sauce

Serves 4

The daikon and cucumber in this recipe are perfect for summertime: cooling, crunchy, and fresh tasting. The *mitsuba*, an herb that has a wonderful, delicate flavor that's a bit like chervil, adds another refreshing note and doesn't overpower. Add tangy yuzu and rich salmon and you have a balanced, nutritious, and delicious dish you can knock out in 15 minutes, from start to finish. If you'd like, you can substitute canned salmon for the fillets and avoid firing up the oven altogether.

4 (4-ounce) salmon fillets

Pinch of kosher salt

Pinch of pepper

12 ounces dried somen noodles

12 cherry tomatoes, halved

¼ cup diced daikon

¼ cup diced cucumber

1 cup Yuzu Dipping Sauce (page 86)

8 stems mitsuba, cut into 1-inch pieces (or substitute with daikon sprouts or cilantro)

Heat a grill or grill pan over high heat. Season the salmon fillets with the salt and pepper, then grill the salmon until medium-rare, 2 to 3 minutes per side.

Place a pot of water over high heat and bring to a boil. Add the somen noodles and cook, following package instructions. Rinse the noodles well under cold running water, drain, and divide among 4 bowls.

Top each bowl with one-fourth of the tomatoes, daikon, and cucumber. Place a salmon fillet in each bowl and drizzle ¼ cup yuzu sauce over it. Garnish with the *mitsuba*.

Somen in a Clay Pot with Chicken and Eggplant

Serves 4

Although somen is typically a summertime food, here's a delicious, fragrant dish you can enjoy year-round. I love cooking with traditional clay pots, which add a nice homey touch. They also keep food warm and, best of all, make a dramatic presentation—especially when you lift the lid to release this dish's seductive aroma. You can find these vessels (called "donabe" in Japanese) in Asian markets, or you can substitute a Dutch oven or any sturdy pot with a lid (enamel or cast-iron pots work great). If you're using a pot, combine all the servings and set the pot, covered, on a heatproof dish on your dining table. Remove the lid with a flourish and ladle into bowls. You'll see that I call for an udon broth for this recipe. So why not udon noodles? Chicken and eggplant are lighter foods that perfectly complement the lighter somen noodle, while the udon broth adds body and flavor to this hot dish. I use violet-colored Chinese eggplants, which are about the size of zucchini and cook quicker than the larger, more common varieties.

2 Chinese eggplants

2 teaspoons vegetable oil

13 ounces chicken leg and thigh, skin on, deboned

Pinch of kosher salt

Pinch of pepper

¼ cup sake

8 pea pods, stemmed

5 cups hot Udon Broth (page 66)

12 ounces dried somen noodles

1¼ cups shimeji mushrooms

½ teaspoon yuzu pepper (optional)

Heat a grill or grill pan until hot. With the tip of a paring knife, poke several small holes on each side of the eggplants. Grill the eggplants, turning every 2 to 4 minutes, until the skin becomes charred and very soft, about 10 minutes total cooking time. Remove the eggplants from the grill and let them sit at room temperature until cool.

Meanwhile, pour the vegetable oil into a pot that is just large enough to place the chicken in a single layer and set it over high heat. Season the chicken with the salt and pepper. When the oil just begins to smoke, add the chicken, skin side down, and cook until the skin turns golden brown, about 2 minutes. Turn the chicken over and cook for 1 minute longer, then flip again and decrease the heat to low.

Carefully pour in the sake, then cover the pot with a lid. Cook over low heat for 2 minutes longer, then remove the pot from the burner and let sit, covered, for 2 minutes. Remove the cooked chicken from the pot and set on a plate or cutting board until cool, then use your hands to shred the chicken into small pieces.

Once the eggplants have cooled, slice off the top and bottom ends and use your hands to peel off the skin, which you can discard. Slice the eggplants in half lengthwise, then into 1-inch-long pieces. Set aside.

Prepare an ice bath and place a pot of water over high heat. When the water comes to a boil, add the pea pods and cook for 45 seconds. Remove the pea pods and submerge in the ice bath. Drain well. When chilled, slice each into ½-inch pieces. Set aside. (Note: Do not discard the boiling water; cover and keep warm until you're ready to cook the noodles.)

Pour the hot broth into 4 clay pots, then set each pot over high heat.

Add the somen noodles to the reserved boiling water and cook until al dente, about 1 minute. Rinse under cold running water until chilled, and drain well.

Once the broth comes to a boil, divide the somen noodles equally among the clay pots and top each with one-fourth of the eggplant, mushrooms, and chicken. Cover and increase the heat to high until the liquid returns to a boil, about 30 seconds. Turn off the heat.

Set a folded paper towel in the center of 2 heatproof plates and rest the clay pots on top of them. Briefly remove the lids to garnish with the pea pods and yuzu pepper. Replace the lids to serve.

Chilled Seafood Somen

Serves 4

Here is an elegant summertime recipe that you can pull together quickly, with minimum time at the stove. You can use fresh or canned crabmeat, and fresh or frozen shrimp and squid. My local supermarket sells frozen squid that has already been cleaned, which is what I use when I cook this dish at home. The sweetness of the seafood in this recipe pairs nicely with the tomato dipping sauce, while the arugula adds a nice contrasting zing.

12 large shrimp, peeled and deveined, with tails on
4 pieces squid, cleaned
1¼ cups Tomato Dipping Sauce (page 86)
14 ounces dried somen noodles
1⅓ cups arugula
½ cup crabmeat, picked over
12 cherry tomatoes, halved
2½ tablespoons chopped toasted pine nuts

Prepare an ice bath and place a pot of heavily salted water over high heat. When the water comes just to a boil, add the shrimp and cook for 2 to 3 minutes, or until cooked through. Remove the shrimp from the water and submerge in the ice bath. Add the squid to the boiling water and cook for 2 minutes, then submerge in the ice bath.

Be careful not to overcook the shrimp and squid, as both will become very tough. Remove the seafood from the ice bath and pat dry. Slice the squid into ¼-inch-thick rings and combine in a small bowl with the shrimp and ¼ cup of the dipping sauce. Mix well and set aside.

Place a pot of water over high heat and bring to a boil. Add the somen noodles and cook, following package instructions. Rinse under cold running water until chilled, then drain well. Divide the noodles equally among 4 plates.

Top each plate of noodles with one-fourth of the arugula, shrimp, squid, and crabmeat. Garnish with the tomatoes and pine nuts and finish by drizzling ¼ cup of the remaining tomato dipping sauce on each plate.

| # Asian Noodles

ASIAN NOODLES

WHILE Thai and Vietnamese rice noodles are now in vogue across Japan, when I was a kid we didn't have Southeast Asian restaurants in my hometown. Only when I moved to Chicago did I first discover these delicacies. I love the aromatic herbs and sweet and spicy tastes of Southeast Asian noodles, so much so that a few years ago I tagged along to Thailand with Chicago's legendary Thai chef Arun Sampanthavivat to taste them at the source. I'll never forget that trip—and the amazing noodles I ate there. In this section I include classic Southeast Asian dishes, such as Pad Thai (page 105) and Curry Shrimp Rice Noodles (page 99), as well as a recipe inspired by the Windy City (page 102).

Another kind of noodle I'm crazy about is mung bean threads, which have a wonderful chewy texture and readily absorb flavors from the dishes they're cooked in. Called *harusame* or *saifun* noodles, they're a favorite in China, Taiwan, Korea, and Japan. Both bean thread noodle recipes in this section are hot and spicy in homage to Korean cooking, which is enormously popular in Japan.

Beef Short Ribs with Saifun Bean Threads

Serves 2

Saifun bean threads are more toothsome and chewier than rice noodles, so they're perfect for stir-frying, like in this recipe. I created this recipe for two servings; if you want to prepare it for four, just cook in two batches. I've combined these noodles with a spicy, tangy sauce and delicious beef short ribs.

2 bunches (3 ounces total) saifun bean threads

SHORT RIBS

1 clove garlic, grated

1 teaspoon sesame oil

1 tablespoon Japanese soy sauce

1 teaspoon sake

1 teaspoon sugar

1/8 teaspoon hot chili oil

Pinch of pepper

12 ounces 1/2-inch-thick bone-in short ribs, cut into 8 pieces

VEGETABLES

1/4 cup dried wood ear mushrooms

1/2 cup stemmed thinly sliced shiitake mushrooms

1/3 cup peeled thinly sliced celery (2-inch lengths)

1/4 cup peeled thinly sliced carrots (2-inch lengths)

1 cup sliced napa cabbage, ends trimmed

SAUCE

2 tablespoons mirin

3 tablespoons Japanese soy sauce

1 tablespoon sunchang kochujang (Korean chili paste)

1 tablespoon hoisin sauce

1 tablespoon sugar

1 tablespoon vegetable oil

2 tablespoons sesame oil

Pinch each of salt and pepper

Place a large pot of water over high heat and bring to a boil. Add the noodles. Turn off the heat and let the noodles sit for 20 minutes, or until they are cooked through. Drain well through a fine-mesh sieve and set aside.

To prepare the short ribs, combine the garlic, sesame oil, soy sauce, sake, sugar, chili oil, and pepper in a large bowl. Mix well. Add the short ribs and turn to coat. Cover and refrigerate for 20 minutes.

While the short ribs are marinating, **prepare the vegetables.** Cover the wood ear mushrooms with the hot water and let them soak for 10 minutes at room temperature. Drain the water and thinly slice the mushrooms. Combine with the rest of the vegetables in a bowl and set aside.

To make the sauce, combine all the ingredients in a small bowl and set aside.

To cook, place a large pan over high heat. Add the vegetable oil. When the oil just begins to smoke, add the short ribs one at a time and cook for 1 minute. Use tongs to turn the ribs over and cook for 1 minute longer, or until the ribs are cooked through. Remove the ribs from the pan, set them on a plate, and cover to keep warm until ready to serve.

Drain the oil from the pan and wipe it clean with a paper towel. Place the pan over high heat and add the sesame oil. Add all the vegetables and cook for 2 minutes, stirring constantly.

(continued)

Reduce the heat to medium and add the noodles to the pan. Cook for 1 minute, then stir in the sauce and season with the salt and pepper. Cook for 4 minutes longer, then remove the pan from the heat.

To serve, divide the noodles and vegetables between 2 plates and top each with 4 short ribs.

Slow-Cooked Oxtails with Rice Noodles

Serves 4

Oxtail is a favorite ingredient in countries as diverse as Jamaica, France, and Korea. When you taste it, it's not hard to understand why. To release oxtail's rich, sublime flavors, though, you must slowly braise it for hours until the meat is absolutely tender. It's worth the wait.

2 pounds oxtails (4 to 8 pieces)

6 cups water

6 cups Dashi (page 40)

2 tablespoons Japanese soy sauce

2 tablespoons sake

Kosher salt

Pinch of pepper

1 cup peeled thinly sliced daikon (each slice halved)

8 ounces dried rice noodles

2 tablespoons thinly sliced jalapeño rounds

2 scallions, both white and green parts, thinly sliced on an angle

4 sprigs cilantro

Combine the oxtails and water in a small saucepan and place over high heat. Bring the water just to a boil, then remove the pot from the heat, drain the water, and rinse the oxtails and pot well.

Return the oxtails to the pot and add the dashi. Set the pot over high heat and bring to a boil. Decrease the heat to low and cover the pot. Simmer the liquid until the meat falls off the bone, about 5 hours. While cooking, add more water, if necessary, to keep the oxtails fully submerged.

When the meat has finished cooking, remove the oxtails from the pot and set them aside. Skim the fat off the top of the broth, discard, and strain the broth into a liquid measuring cup. Measure 6 cups of broth, adding water, if necessary, to equal 6 cups. Pour the broth into a pot and bring to a boil, then add the soy sauce, sake, salt to taste, and pepper. Decrease the heat to low and return the oxtails to the pot. Cover the pot to keep warm until you're ready to serve.

Place a large pot of water over high heat and bring to a boil. Add the daikon and simmer for 5 minutes. Use tongs or a slotted spoon to transfer the daikon from the water to the warm broth. (Do not drain the water.)

Return the water to a boil, add the rice noodles, and cook following package instructions. Drain well and divide among 4 bowls.

Pour 1½ cups of the broth into each bowl and add one-fourth of the oxtails. Garnish with the jalapeño, scallions, and cilantro.

Curry Shrimp Rice Noodles

Serves 2

I tasted an unforgettable version of this dish on a trip to Thailand a few years ago, in the city of Chiang Mai, which is famous for its vibrant Thai curries. I love the mixture of aromatic flavors and textures here, and the way this dish is sweet, pungent, and spicy all at once. If you can find them, use Thai eggplants, which are a pale green in color, and have a nice, delicate flavor. Or you can substitute slender Chinese eggplants. This dish has a lot of ingredients but is very straightforward and easy to prepare.

2 tablespoons vegetable oil

1 clove garlic, thinly sliced

½ teaspoon grated ginger

½ red onion, thinly sliced

¼ red bell pepper, thinly sliced

1 tablespoon curry powder

2½ cups chicken broth

½ cup coconut milk

1 tablespoon Thai curry paste

2 tablespoons nam pla (fish sauce)

1 teaspoon rice wine vinegar

2 kaffir lime leaves

Pinch each of salt and pepper

8 (½-inch-thick) Thai eggplant slices

5 ounces dried rice noodles

8 large shrimp, peeled and deveined, with tails off

Put the oil in a large sauté pan and set over medium heat. Once the pan is hot, add the garlic, ginger, red onion, and bell pepper and cook, stirring often, until the vegetables become soft, 4 to 5 minutes. Mix in the curry powder and cook until it is well absorbed, about 1 minute. Then add the chicken broth, coconut milk, Thai curry paste, nam pla, rice wine vinegar, kaffir lime leaves, and salt and pepper. Mix well and add the eggplant. Simmer for 15 to 20 minutes, until the eggplant is tender and the chicken is cooked through. Remove the kaffir lime leaves and discard.

Place a large pot of water over high heat and bring to a boil. Add the rice noodles and cook, following package instructions.

While the noodles are cooking, add the shrimp to the simmering broth. Cook for 2 to 3 minutes, or until the shrimp are cooked through.

To serve, drain the noodles and divide between 2 bowls. Top each with 4 shrimp and half the sauce and vegetables.

Cassoulet of Crab, Kimchi, and Harusame

Serves 4

This dish was inspired by Korean cooking, which is extremely popular in Japan. With a hearty and spicy broth, it's perfect for wintertime, when crabs are at their peak flavor. I like to serve this dish in individual Asian hot pot dishes, but you can also combine this recipe into one big pot and ladle into bowls. If you're using live crabs, be sure to remove the head, gills, and tough outer shells before cooking.

1½ tablespoons sesame oil

4 blue crabs, cleaned and quartered (frozen or live)

2 cloves garlic, thinly sliced

5 cups Dashi (page 40)

2 tablespoons sake

2 tablespoons Japanese soy sauce

1 cup roughly chopped kimchi

¼ cup red or brown miso

1 teaspoon kosher salt

8 ounces dried harusame (mung bean thread noodles)

2 ounces (1 cup) shungiku (chrysanthemum leaves), ends trimmed

2 scallions, both white and green parts, thinly sliced on an angle

Place a pot over high heat and add the sesame oil. After 1 minute, add the crabs and cook until they turn bright red-orange, about 3 minutes. Then stir in the garlic and cook until it begins to turn light brown, about 30 seconds more.

Add the dashi and bring just to a boil. Decrease the heat and simmer for 3 minutes. Skim the surface of the liquid if necessary to remove any scum produced by the crabs.

Stir in the sake, soy sauce, kimchi, miso paste, and salt, and simmer for 3 minutes. Reduce the heat to low and keep warm until ready to serve.

Place a pot of water over high heat and bring to a boil. Add the noodles and cook, following package directions. Rinse well under cold running water and drain. Lay the noodles in a loose pile on a cutting board and cut into quarters.

Fill each of 4 small Asian hot pot dishes or cassoulet dishes with the noodles and set them over high heat. Divide the crab and broth among the hot pots and cover. Bring the broth to a boil, about 3 minutes, then add the *shungiku*. Cover again and cook until the *shungiku* just becomes tender, 1 to 2 minutes longer. Garnish with the scallions and serve hot.

Corned Beef with Rice Noodles

Serves 4

Credit my Irish-Italian, Chicago-native wife, Kathy, for inspiring this dish. She loves corned beef, a Windy City favorite, so I've cooked it many times for my family. But I've always thought it was a shame that we enjoyed the delicious brisket but ignored the flavorful cooking broth, which typically isn't consumed. So I thought, look at it the Japanese way—add noodles. I tried it and it tasted fantastic. So now when I make corned beef, my Irish-Italian-Japanese children always look forward to corned beef broth noodles with leftovers the next day. This dish takes time to cook slowly, but it's easy to prepare. You can also use leftover corned beef for hash and sandwiches.

2 to 3 pounds uncooked corned beef brisket and packaged spice mix (brisket and spice mix come packaged at the grocery store)

¼ onion, peeled and ends trimmed

1 stalk celery, peeled and cut into 1-inch pieces

1 carrot, peeled and cut into 1-inch pieces

½ green cabbage, core removed and halved

1 leek, white part only, halved lengthwise

⅛ teaspoon red pepper flakes

1 bay leaf

1 tablespoon Japanese soy sauce

10 ounces dried rice noodles

Grainy Dijon mustard, for garnish

Cut the beef in half and place both pieces in a large pot. Fill with enough cold water to cover the beef. Turn the heat to high and bring the water just to a boil, then strain the liquid and discard. Return the beef to the pot and cover again with cold water. Set over high heat until the water comes to a boil, then decrease the heat and simmer for 1½ to 2 hours.

Transfer the meat to a new pot and strain the cooking liquid through a fine-mesh sieve. Cover the meat with the strained cooking liquid and return to a simmer. Add the packaged spice mix, onion, celery, carrot, cabbage, leek, red pepper flakes, bay leaf, and soy sauce; cook for 30 minutes, or until the beef is very tender. Test for doneness by inserting a paring knife into the center of the beef; it's done if the knife slides easily into the meat. Remove the bay leaf and discard.

Remove one piece of corned beef and place it on a cutting board. Slice into ¼-inch-thick pieces. Reserve the other piece of corned beef for future use.

Place a large pot of water over high heat and bring to a boil. Add the rice noodles and cook, following package instructions. Drain well and divide among 4 bowls.

To serve, fill each of the bowls with one-fourth of the sliced beef, onion, celery, carrot, cabbage, and leek, and ¼ cup of the cooking broth. Garnish with a dab of mustard.

IDEAS FOR LEFTOVER CORNED BEEF

This recipe makes more corned beef than you need for this dish. You can use leftover corned beef the way we do in Chicago: turn it into a sandwich. Pile slices on crusty bread, garnish with the cooked cabbage and carrot, then slather on mustard. And don't forget corned beef hash! Shred the corned beef and stir fry it with diced potatoes and onions. Season with salt and pepper and serve with eggs. Not Japanese, of course, but both delicious.

Grilled Pork with Green Papaya Salad and Rice Noodles

Serves 4

This Southeast Asian–influenced dish is perfect for summer dining: it is light and refreshing, with tangy sweet-and-sour flavors. I love green papaya, an ingredient that has an appealing crunch and natural sweetness. Lemongrass, another one of my favorite Southeast Asian ingredients, adds a wonderful lemony fragrance. I cook with both at my restaurant.

PORK MARINADE

1 teaspoon grated ginger

1 teaspoon grated garlic

1 (8-inch) piece lemongrass, halved and smashed

¼ cup Japanese soy sauce

2 teaspoons sesame oil

4 teaspoons sake

Pinch each of salt and pepper

4 teaspoons sugar

12 ounces pork loin, thinly sliced

GREEN PAPAYA SALAD

¼ cup thinly sliced red onion

¼ cup thinly sliced jicama

¼ cup thinly sliced cucumber

½ cup thinly sliced green papaya

DRESSING

6 tablespoons rice wine vinegar

2 tablespoons sugar

2 teaspoons tobanjan (Chinese chili paste)

1 teaspoon nam pla (fish sauce)

10 ounces dried rice noodles

4 cups butter lettuce or other leafy greens

4 sprigs cilantro

4 teaspoons chopped toasted peanuts

To make the marinade, combine all the ingredients in a bowl. Add the pork and mix well. Cover and refrigerate for 20 minutes.

In the meantime, to prepare the green papaya salad, place all the ingredients in a bowl and toss to combine.

To prepare the dressing, place all the ingredients in a small bowl and whisk to combine. Drizzle over the salad and toss to combine thoroughly.

Heat a grill or grill pan over high heat. Add the pork and cook on each side for 1 minute, or until cooked through. Transfer the pork to a plate and cover to keep warm.

Place a large pot of water over high heat and bring to a boil. Add the rice noodles and cook, following package instructions. Drain well.

To assemble, arrange 1 cup of lettuce on each of 4 plates. Divide the noodles among the plates and place on top of the lettuce. Add one-fourth of the green papaya salad and pork to each plate. Garnish with the cilantro and toasted peanuts.

Pad Thai

Serves 2

One of Thailand's signature dishes, pad thai is as popular in Japan as it is here in America. Rice noodles are easy to overcook, so be sure to prepare this dish in small batches. If you do want to serve four people, prepare enough ingredients for four servings (including doubling the sauce), but cook the recipe in two batches, one after the other. Also, use a nonstick skillet, if possible, because rice noodles can stick to a regular pan.

3 tablespoons peanuts

¼ cup dehydrated shrimp (available in Asian markets)

½ cup hot water

2 tablespoons nam pla (fish sauce)

1 teaspoon tobanjan (Chinese chili paste)

1 tablespoon sugar

1 teaspoon rice vinegar

Pinch each of salt and pepper

5 ounces dried rice noodles

3 tablespoons vegetable oil

6 large shrimp, peeled and deveined, with tails off

6 ounces pork loin, thinly sliced

1 clove garlic, minced

2 cups bean sprouts

½ cup chopped garlic chives (1-inch pieces)

2 eggs, beaten

2 sprigs cilantro

Preheat the oven to 350°F. Lay the peanuts on a baking sheet and roast in the oven until lightly toasted, about 5 minutes. Remove from the oven and let cool at room temperature, then roughly chop. Set aside.

Place the dehydrated shrimp in a small bowl. Cover with the hot water and let sit at room temperature for 10 minutes. Drain well and chop into small pieces. Set aside

In a bowl, mix together the nam pla, *tobanjan*, sugar, vinegar, and salt and pepper. Set aside.

Place a large pot of water over high heat and bring to a boil. Add the rice noodles and cook, following package instructions. Drain the noodles and rinse well under cold running water. Toss the noodles with 1 tablespoon of the vegetable oil to prevent them from sticking together. Set aside.

Place a large nonstick sauté pan over medium-high heat. Add the remaining 2 tablespoons oil and heat for 30 seconds. Add the 6 large shrimp and cook for 30 seconds. Stir in the pork and cook for 2 minutes longer, stirring frequently. Using a slotted spoon, transfer the shrimp and pork to a plate, leaving behind the cooking oil. Set aside.

Return the pan to the burner and decrease the heat to medium. Add the garlic and cook for 15 seconds, then stir in the rehydrated shrimp, peanuts, bean sprouts, and garlic chives, and cook for 1 minute. Add the eggs and cook for 30 seconds, then turn off the heat but keep the pan on the burner. Stir in the noodles and reserved pork and shrimp, then add the sauce mixture, combining well.

Turn the heat to high and cook, stirring frequently, until the pork and shrimp are heated through.

Remove the pan from the heat and divide the noodles and vegetables between 2 plates. Garnish with a few cilantro leaves.

Rice Noodle Pho

Serves 4

This light and flavorful noodle dish is one of my favorites. We use a lot of Asian ingredients at my Chicago restaurant, foods I shop for myself at the local Asian market. The best part of those trips is the Vietnamese place next door, where I stop regularly, shopping bags in hand, for a delicious bowl of *pho* before heading back to my kitchen. Lightly dipping the beef in broth to cook it, as I describe below, is referred to as "shabu-shabu" in Japan.

6 cups beef broth (page 107)

1 cinnamon stick

4 pieces star anise

8 ounces beef sirloin or rib eye, thinly sliced (ask your butcher to slice it very thin)

½ red onion, thinly sliced

¼ cup nam pla (fish sauce)

1 tablespoon shirojoyu (white soy sauce)

¼ teaspoon kosher salt

Pinch of pepper

10 ounces dried rice noodles

2 cups bean sprouts

12 basil leaves

8 sprigs cilantro

2 teaspoons garlic oil (recipe follows)

Combine the beef broth, cinnamon, and star anise in a saucepan and bring to a boil over high heat. Reduce the heat to medium and simmer for 4 minutes. Remove the spices from the liquid and discard.

Dip each piece of beef, one at a time, into the simmering broth for 10 seconds, and then set on a plate. Repeat until you've dipped all the beef slices. Cover the plate when done to keep warm.

Once all the beef has been cooked, add the onion, nam pla, and *shirojoyu* to the broth. Season to taste with the salt and pepper. Decrease the heat to low and keep warm until ready to serve.

Place a pot of water over high heat and bring to a boil. Add the rice noodles and cook, following the package instructions. Drain well and divide the noodles among 4 bowls.

To serve, top each bowl of noodles with 1½ cups broth and one-fourth of the beef. Garnish with the bean sprouts, basil leaves, cilantro, and garlic oil.

GARLIC OIL AND GARLIC CHIPS

Makes 1 cup

1 cup extra-virgin olive oil

2 tablespoons thinly sliced garlic

Pour the oil into a small sauté pan and place over medium heat. Add the garlic and carefully stir with a wooden spoon. Cook for 6 to 8 minutes, or until the garlic just begins to turn golden brown and become crisp. Be careful not to overcook the garlic, or both the garlic chips and the oil will become bitter.

Strain the oil through a fine-mesh sieve and let cool at room temperature. Carefully transfer the garlic chips to a paper towel to cool. Use them as a garnish for Mushroom Ramen (page 20).

Takashi's Noodles

Beef Broth

Makes 2 quarts

If you happen to live near a butcher shop, ask them for scrap meat, the pieces that usually go to make ground beef. Otherwise, pick up stew meat at the supermarket to prepare this broth—no need to cook this recipe with expensive cuts of beef.

3 pounds beef scrap meat or stew meat

6 quarts cold water

1 cup peeled chopped carrots

1 cup chopped celery

1 cup chopped onion

1 cup chopped leek (white part only)

2 cloves garlic, smashed

1 (1-inch) piece ginger, peeled and smashed

Combine the beef and 3 quarts of the water in a large pot and place over high heat. Bring to a boil, then turn off the heat and drain the liquid through a sieve (discard the liquid). Rinse the beef and the pot well with cold water to remove any impurities, then return the beef to the pot again and cover with the remaining 3 quarts cold water.

Bring the water to a boil again, then decrease the heat to medium so the liquid simmers. Skim the surface to remove any scum that has accumulated. Add the carrots, celery, onion, leek, garlic, and ginger, and simmer for 2 to 3 hours to extract as much beef flavor as possible. The broth will reduce while it simmers, making 2 quarts when finished. Drain through a fine-mesh sieve and discard the beef and vegetables.

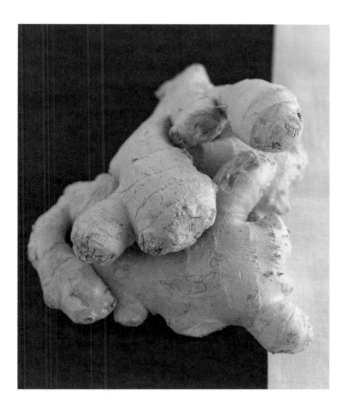

CHAPTER SIX | Pasta

PASTA

SPAGHETTI as *Japanese* food? I first tasted Italian pasta in high school when I worked in the kitchen of a European-style restaurant, which introduced me to Bolognese, Neapolitan, and other classic sauces. But Italian pasta is more than just a foreign import in Japan—it's so popular that it has been adopted into the local cuisine. You can find "Japanese-Italian" restaurants across the country serving surprising combinations such as spaghetti with clams and seaweed, and orecchiette with shiitake, enoki, and shimeji mushrooms. These dishes are almost unknown here in America, but the melding of Italian pasta with clean Japanese flavors is a natural.

It is believed that a French missionary built the first macaroni factory in Japan in the late nineteenth century during the Meiji Restoration. The Japanese became interested in Western-style food during this time, a period in history when Japan opened its doors to the world after two hundred years of isolation. Japanese emissaries were sent to Europe and America to learn their ways, and were shocked to discover how much shorter they were than Westerners! Emperor Meiji believed that Japanese eating had to be changed to counter this, so he encouraged Western food habits, especially the consumption of meat.

Fast-forward to modern times, when in the late 1970s to early '80s, Japan experienced what is called the "Pasta Boom." Italian pasta took off, and so did "*wafu*" pasta, that is, "Japanese-style" pasta.

The recipes in this section include classic *wafu* pasta dishes, as well as many of my own delicious and elegant creations, dishes that reflect my two decades of cooking in America, and my fascination with matching Japanese ingredients and flavors to Western cooking. Given how much I love noodles, it's only natural that Italian pasta has been such an inspiring culinary canvas for me.

Egg Pasta

Serves 4

This is the master recipe for egg pasta to accompany three dishes in the book: Squid-Ink Pasta with Crabmeat-Stuffed Squid (page 124), Fresh Egg Pasta with Seared Lamb (page 109), and Fresh Egg Pasta with Pork Loin (page 128). Adding squid ink to this recipe turns the pasta almost black and makes a dramatic presentation. It adds a subtle ocean flavor to a dish that's absolutely sublime. I first started preparing squid-ink pasta at Ambria Restaurant, the legendary Chicago fine dining restaurant where I cooked for nine years.

2 cups all-purpose flour, plus more for dusting

2 eggs

1 tablespoon extra-virgin olive oil

1 teaspoon squid ink (optional)

1 teaspoon kosher salt

3 tablespoons water

Form the 2 cups flour into a small mound on a clean work surface. Make a hole in the center of it. Pour in the eggs, olive oil, squid ink, salt, and 1½ tablespoons of the water, and gradually incorporate with the flour using a fork. Continue incorporating until well combined. Add more of the remaining 1½ tablespoons water as necessary.

With your hands, work in any remaining flour. Form the dough into a ball. Lightly flatten the ball and, with the heel of your hand, begin kneading by working the bottom of the dough over the top. Rotate the dough a quarter turn and repeat. Continue doing this until all the dough is no longer sticky. Cover the dough with plastic wrap and let it sit at room temperature for 30 minutes.

Divide the dough into 4 equal pieces. Gently flatten and dust one piece of dough with flour. Cover the remaining dough with plastic to prevent it from drying out. Assemble a countertop pasta roller and adjust the settings of the roller to the widest setting, usually #1. Dust the roller with flour as well.

Begin rolling the dough by turning the hand crank while feeding the dough through the opening in the roller. Fold the dough in half and repeat four more times, folding the dough in half each time. After five turns through the roller, shape the dough into a rectangle and roll it two more times. Dust with flour as needed to keep the dough from sticking to the roller.

Adjust the roller to setting #2 and roll the dough through one time. Do the same at settings #3 and #4, continuing to dust with flour as needed. When you get to setting #5, roll the dough twice and then set aside. The dough should now be at least 12 inches long. Repeat the process with the remaining dough to end up with 4 long, flat pieces.

Assemble the pasta cutter attachment to the roller. While cranking, feed the dough through the spaghetti cutter. Two-thirds of the way through, release the dough from the hand you're using to feed it and move your hand beneath the roller to gently gather the cut noodles. Continue cranking. Once the entire sheet of pasta has been cut, lightly dust the noodles with flour and lay them flat on a floured tray. Repeat with the remaining dough.

To cook the noodles, bring a large pot of salted water to a boil. Cook the noodles in the water, stirring often, for 2 minutes, or until the noodles are cooked through. Drain well and serve with your favorite sauce.

Angel Hair Pasta with Steamed Chicken

Serves 4

The secret to this cool, summertime dish? Steaming the chicken. When you steam chicken, it stays moist and juicy even if you serve it cold. And caramelizing the skin beforehand adds lots of wonderful flavor. These are both techniques I borrow from Chinese cuisine. The angel hair pasta in this dish plays the same role as somen noodles: not too chewy or overwhelming when enjoyed cold.

2 tablespoons vegetable oil

4 chicken thighs, boned

Salt and pepper

¼ cup sake

12 ounces dried angel hair pasta

1½ cups peeled and thinly sliced English cucumbers

8 cherry tomatoes, quartered

4 umeboshi (pickled Japanese apricots), pitted and chopped into a paste

8 obha leaves, ends trimmed and very thinly sliced

½ teaspoon spicy mustard (Asian hot mustard)

1½ cups Cold Soba Broth (page 41)

Place a heavy-bottomed pot over high heat. Add the oil. Season the chicken with salt and pepper to taste. When the oil just begins to smoke, add the chicken, skin side down, and cook until the skin turns golden brown, 3 to 4 minutes. Drain the oil, leaving the chicken in the pot, and return it to high heat. Turn the chicken thighs over and add the sake. Decrease the heat to low and cover the pot to steam. Cook for 4 minutes, or until the chicken is cooked through. Remove the chicken from the pot and refrigerate until cool, about 20 minutes. Once the chicken has cooled, slice very thin. Set aside.

Place a large pot of salted water over high heat and bring to a boil. Add the angel hair pasta and cook, following package instructions. Once cooked through, rinse the pasta well under cold running water until the noodles are cold. Drain and divide among 4 shallow bowls.

Top each bowl of pasta with one-fourth of the cucumbers, then the chicken, cherry tomatoes, umeboshi, *obha* leaves, mustard, and cold soba broth. Enjoy cold.

Chilled Penne with Tuna and Japanese Mushrooms

Serves 4

This is my wife, Kathy, and my "S.O.S." dish—the one we rely on when we have to whip up something fast and elegant with minimal cooking. You can prepare this recipe in about 20 minutes, but you won't skimp on taste: with mushrooms, Dijon, tuna, and chives, there are layers of wonderful flavor here, and the richness of the dish complements the cold pasta.

½ cup stemmed and halved enoki mushrooms

1 cup shimeji mushrooms, ends trimmed

2 tablespoons kosher salt

12 ounces dried penne

⅓ cup mayonnaise

1½ teaspoons Dijon mustard

1½ teaspoons lemon juice

⅛ teaspoon pepper

¾ teaspoon sugar

1 (6-ounce) can of tuna packed in oil, drained, oil reserved

1 stalk celery, peeled and thinly sliced on a 1-inch-long angle

¼ cup thinly sliced red onion (½-inch pieces)

¼ cup packed arugula

1 teaspoon minced chives

Place a large pot of water over high heat, add the salt, and bring to a boil. Put all the mushrooms in a fine-mesh sieve that will fit in the pot. Place the sieve in the pot, making sure the mushrooms are completely submerged in the water. Cook the mushrooms for 30 seconds. Remove the mushrooms and set aside. (Don't discard the cooking water.)

Return the water to a boil. Add the pasta and cook, following package instructions. Once cooked, rinse the pasta under cold running water until chilled, then drain well. Set aside.

Combine the mayonnaise, mustard, lemon juice, pepper, sugar, and 1 tablespoon of the reserved tuna oil in a bowl and mix well to make the dressing.

Add ¼ cup of the dressing to the cooked pasta. Mix until the pasta is evenly coated, salting to taste, then divide the pasta among 4 plates.

In another bowl, combine the tuna, mushrooms, celery, and onion with the remaining dressing. Top the pasta with the tuna and vegetables, then garnish with the arugula and minced chives.

Fresh Egg Pasta with Seared Lamb, Asian Vegetables, and Sweet Soy-Ginger Sauce

Serves 4

To tell you the truth, I first created this dish by accident, when I added lamb instead of beef by mistake. But when I tasted it, I realized it was no mistake! Lamb might not be a traditional Japanese ingredient, but it's delicious when mixed with these Asian flavors and vegetables. If you prefer beef, though, you can always use that instead. Follow the fresh Egg Pasta recipe on page 109, but leave out the optional squid ink.

SWEET SOY-GINGER SAUCE

½ teaspoon grated garlic

1 teaspoon grated ginger

½ cup Japanese soy sauce

½ cup mirin

4 teaspoons sesame oil

1 teaspoon tobanjan (Chinese chili paste)

25 pea pods, stemmed, veins removed

1 pound Egg Pasta (page 109; omit optional squid ink) or spaghetti

2 tablespoons vegetable oil

1 pound lamb shoulder chop, thinly sliced

3 cups stemmed chopped napa cabbage

20 pieces canned baby corn, halved lengthwise

3 cups stemmed sliced shiitake mushrooms

2 cups sliced onion

3 cups bean sprouts

Pinch of pepper

To make the sauce, combine all the ingredients in a small bowl. Mix well and set aside.

Prepare an ice bath and place a large pot of salted water over high heat. When the water comes to a boil, add the pea pods and cook for 1 minute. Remove the pea pods and submerge in the ice bath (don't discard the cooking water). Once cool (about 30 seconds), pat the pea pods dry. Cut in half and set aside.

Return the water to a boil and stir in the pasta. At the same time, place a very large sauté pan over high heat and add the vegetable oil. Once the oil just begins to smoke, add the lamb and cook on one side for 30 seconds, then flip the lamb over and stir in the cabbage, baby corn, mushrooms, and onion. Cook for 2 minutes. By this time, the pasta should be cooked through (be careful not to overcook). Drain the pasta and add it to the sauté pan along with the reserved soy-ginger sauce. Mix well, then add the bean sprouts and pepper. Cook for 30 seconds longer, or until the bean sprouts are warm.

Remove the pan from the heat. Divide the noodles, lamb, and vegetables among 4 plates and serve.

Onsen Tamago Pasta

Serves 4

This rich, delicious dish is my twist on classic pasta carbonara. But instead of raw eggs, I prepare it with *onsen tamago*, which I think makes it more interesting. What's *onsen tamago*? It literally translates to "hot spring eggs," which means the egg whites are soft and still runny, but the yolks have a creamy consistency, resembling soft-boiled eggs. It is a standard breakfast treat at the countless hot springs that dot Japan. Since I was young I've loved eggs cooked this way. The keys to preparing them are timing and temperature—both have to be exact. Also, the raw egg has to be cold, so be sure to keep the eggs in the refrigerator until the moment you're ready to cook.

4 eggs

12 ounces dried linguine

2 cups sliced bacon

2 cloves garlic, sliced

Pinch of red pepper flakes

1²/₃ cups heavy cream

1¹/₃ cups grated Parmesan cheese

Pinch each of salt and pepper

2 tablespoons unsalted butter

2 tablespoons minced parsley

Prepare an ice bath and place a large pot of salted water over medium-high heat. Using a kitchen thermometer, bring the water to 180°F. Add the eggs and cook for 13 minutes, keeping the water as close to 180°F as possible. At that 13-minute mark, the eggs will be cooked through, so remove them and submerge them in the ice bath (be sure to keep the cooking water, and not drain it). Once cool, remove the eggs from the ice bath and set aside.

Return the same pot of water to a boil and stir in the linguine. Cook according to the package instructions.

While the pasta is cooking, place a large sauté pan over medium heat. Add the bacon and cook, stirring often, until it's crisp, about 6 minutes. Stir in the garlic and red pepper flakes and cook for 1 minute longer. Add the cream and let it come to a boil, then decrease the heat to low and simmer for 1 minute. Remove the pan from the heat and set aside.

When the pasta is almost finished cooking, add the eggs (still in their shells) to the water to reheat for 1 minute. Drain the pasta and set aside the eggs.

Add the pasta to the sauté pan with the sauce and combine well. Increase the heat to high. Mix in the Parmesan cheese, salt, pepper, and butter, and cook until the butter has melted. Add the parsley and toss until it is well combined.

To serve, divide the pasta with sauce among 4 plates. The eggs should be just cool enough to handle by now, so gently tap them on the counter to break the shells. For each one, peel off half of the eggshell and scoop out the egg with a spoon. Place an egg on top of each plate of pasta. Serve warm.

Spaghetti Bolognese

Serves 4

I still remember the first time I tasted this dish. I was sixteen years old and working my first cooking job to earn some pocket money at a restaurant in my hometown that served European food. Until then, I had almost no exposure to Western cooking (I hadn't even tried pizza yet!). This dish was a bit of a culture shock for me, but I quickly became enchanted with Italian pasta. For the recipe, you can substitute ground veal or ground pork, if you like. Any leftover sauce can be frozen for up to a month.

¼ cup extra-virgin olive oil

8 ounces ground beef

2 tablespoons minced garlic

1 onion, minced (about 1¼ cups)

¾ cup full-bodied red wine, such as Merlot or
    Cabernet Sauvignon

3 Roma tomatoes, cored and chopped (about 1½ cups)

¾ cup tomato juice

¼ cup tomato paste

1 sprig fresh thyme

1 bay leaf

3 tablespoons unsalted butter

3 tablespoons grated Parmesan cheese, plus more for garnish

1 tablespoon honey

1 teaspoon balsamic vinegar

12 ounces dried spaghetti

1½ tablespoons kosher salt

¼ teaspoon pepper

Pinch of nutmeg

Pinch of cayenne pepper

2 tablespoons minced fresh basil leaves

Preheat the oven to 400°F.

Heat 2 tablespoons of the olive oil in an ovenproof pot over medium heat. Add the ground beef and cook, stirring constantly with a wooden spoon, until the beef is cooked through and has broken down into small pieces, 3 to 4 minutes. Drain the beef through a fine-mesh sieve and discard the oil. Set the beef aside.

Set the same pot over low heat and add the remaining 2 tablespoons olive oil. Wait 30 seconds, then add the garlic and cook, stirring frequently, until the garlic turns golden brown, about 1 minute. Stir in the onion and increase the heat to medium-high. Cook, stirring often, until the onion becomes very soft, 10 to 12 minutes.

Return the drained beef to the pot and cook for 1 minute. Add the red wine and simmer until the liquid reduces by half (you should be able to see the bottom of the pot when you drag the spoon through the sauce), about 10 minutes.

Add the chopped tomatoes, tomato juice, tomato paste, thyme, and bay leaf. Cover the pot and place in the oven. Cook for 1½ hours, or until the meat and tomatoes become very soft.

Remove the pot from the oven, uncover, and remove and discard the bay leaf. Return the pot to the stove top over low heat and add the butter, Parmesan cheese, honey,